Dancing with Cancer

"Judy Erel has a survivor personality and shares her experience with us. I have learned from my patients that self-induced healing is not a lucky spontaneous event. It takes courage and the willingness to change yourself and your life so your body gets the message. The wisdom and knowledge that she has learned from her experience with cancer can be our guide and coach. I could write a book just pointing out the wisdom she shares with us. She has learned what healing your life and body is about versus waging a war against cancer. She guides us and shows us the path to healing and how to awaken our body to the joy of life and understand the value and wisdom of our consciousness."

Bernie Siegel MD, Author of Love, Medicine and Miracles *and* The Art of Healing

"I was called to see Judy in 2007, when she was diagnosed with multiple myeloma. From our first encounter, she was full of energy and ready to fight for her life. She had a plan. With her amazing willpower and optimism, she would replace the 'bad' diseased cells in her body with 'smiling' healthy cells. During her third chemotherapy treatment she developed a severe reaction and felt herself slipping away. She willed herself to life and pulled out of it. Side by side with chemotherapy and radiotherapy, and the help of her loving children, Judy utilized all her resources and her artistic gift and 'drew' herself to recovery. Her book will empower travellers setting out in the not so simple and not easy journey from sickness to health."

Dr Naomi Rahimi-Levene, Haematologist and Head of the Blood Bank
Asaf Harofe Hospital Haematological Institute

"In *Dancing with Cancer*, Judy Erel weaves a unique theoretical and practical connection between mind and body that is invaluable. She succeeds in developing a powerful healing language that provides an opportunity for change and simple integration into daily life. As her story and exercises flow across the pages, the reader is taken through a process leading to the awareness of choice in life and a path strengthening the positive and the easy. A must for all therapists and anyone who wants to understand and successfully implement the magic of change."

Ruty Bar MA, Movement Therapist, Senior Trainer in Feldenkrais Method Training programs
and Educational Director

Dancing with Cancer

USING TRANSFORMATIONAL ART, MEDITATION AND
A JOYOUS MINDSET TO FACE THE CHALLENGE

JUDY EREL

WATKINS

Sharing Wisdom Since
1893

To my beloved children, Avital, Yael and Gadi … who always have
been partners in my journey and always have my back

And to my grandkids, Michal, Yonatan and Amit, who fill me
with boundless love and joy

Dancing with Cancer
Judy Erel

First published in the UK and USA in 2018 by
Watkins, an imprint of Watkins Media Limited
19 Cecil Court
London WC2N 4EZ

enquiries@watkinspublishing.com

Design and typography copyright © Watkins Media Limited 2018

Text and artwork copyright © Judy Erel 2018
with the exception of:
Mandala templates and step-by-step mandala drawing instructions on pages 16–17 and 182–187
copyright © Eitan Kedmy 2012, 2018

Designed and typeset by JCS Publishing Services Ltd

A CIP record for this book is available from the British Library

ISBN: 978-1-78678-119-2

1 3 5 7 9 10 8 6 4 2

Typeset in Minion Pro
Colour reproduction by XY Digital
Printed and bound in the United Kingdom

www.watkinspublishing.com

Contents

PART TWO – THOUGHT WORK TOOL BOX

List of Illustrations

Introduction
Beyond Wishful Thinking

This book is about how my life danced to the rhythms of extreme illness, conventional medical protocols and the decision to proactively support the best healing outcomes possible as I faced the life-threatening, life-changing reality of incurable, chronic cancer. My hope is that what I share here can help others find their own best healing possibilities.

My life showed me that cancer was like a roadblock on my life's path, with a sign saying "Continual disharmony straight ahead. It's time to make decisions . . . or not." Although the crossroads and roadblocks may be different for each person, we are all on a journey. Each person has their own personal resources at their disposal along the way. What the journey has shown me is that facing cancer is about taking responsibility for our lives and health, and by doing so, maximizing our potential to heal. It is also about harnessing personal resources in order to actively participate in the healing process. When I speak of resources, this includes our mindset, what we learned in school, at work, through just living, what we like doing, what makes us happy, what balances us and makes us smile.

For me one facet came from studying, teaching and creating art, and another from academic studies and work experience in psychology and cognitive development. And the final piece of the puzzle, which also became the core connecting it all, was my experience as a meditation guide and my deep interest in mind–body–soul interactions, energy healing, art therapy, personal empowerment and a love of dancing.

In short, my life came together to reveal an intuitive path of action – something I thought of as my "golden path". I knew that if I was to survive and really thrive, I needed to honestly and fearlessly unleash the creative power of my thoughts, words and deeds. If I wanted to Dance With Cancer, I had to find the way to take the lead. At times the dance was graceful, at times quite clumsy. Sometimes my dance was rhythmic, and occasionally I danced the dance of a beached whale with excruciating slowness.

As my attention focused on ways to maximize my healing potential, I intuitively slipped into the mindset of responsibility for my cells, my body, my feelings, beliefs and attitudes. Each step of my journey filled with meaning and I felt the glow of my efforts. I deeply understood the well-known Buddhist adage that Haruki Murakami had applied to marathon running: "Pain is inevitable. Suffering is a choice."[1] I had definitely chosen not to suffer, if possible.

As I aimed my thoughts, words and ideas specifically at healing expectations, my intentions turned into practical and expressive actions that were beyond the mere "wishful thinking" of optimism and thinking positively. I sensed that I did things that anchored my physical world to specific, defined targets – aiming as high as I could imagine as I focused on my body, my cells and the body's innate intelligence. Unexpectedly, I found myself in the midst of a truly challenging, fascinating and extreme journey. And I felt that extraordinary feeling, that "rush" of living on the edge and the great joy and gratitude of being alive.

I have written this book to share this experience and in doing so, hope to help others help themselves. The book is divided into two parts:

Part One presents my personal journey from cancer diagnosis through treatment and remission and beyond. At each step, I share practical suggestions that may be suitable to incorporate into your own healing journey. I found that using a journal helped me actively "talk" to myself and reveal my individual path, and therefore I invite you to keep a journal, notebook or a pad of paper at hand to help you along the way. You'll find the practical suggestion sections filled with ideas of self-inquiry, creative and journaling exercises as well as guided meditations to support your efforts.

Part Two is a didactic recap of the verbal and nonverbal tools that I came to call "Thought Work", which is basically a routine of expressing and anchoring thoughts in action. By joining thoughts with actions, Thought Work focuses attention, intention and will (desire) in the now moment to create a mindset that is more than the wishful thinking of a good mood or basic optimism. In this manner, you can foster powerful forces of creation.

I hope you find the processes described in this book to be practical, doable ways to actively participate in your own healing process – in addition to conventional medical procedures and/or other complementary or integrative approaches. Thought Work –

uniting intention and doing – is not a substitute for professional medical care of any kind for anyone, me included.

I wish to stress the fact that I did not choose or use Thought Work instead of medical treatment nor was it a factor in my choice of medical treatments. I personally chose to follow the conventional medical protocols, as suggested by my doctors, as well as some supplemental therapy like energy healing (reiki) and herbs. I see Thought Work as a method for active support to maximize outcomes for all and any treatments and approaches chosen.

NOTE

1. Haruki Murakami, *What I Talk About When I Talk About Running*. London: Vintage Books, 2008; p. vii.

Part One
Dancing Through the Storm

"Life isn't about waiting for the storm to pass . . . It's about learning to dance in the rain."

Vivian Greene

Chapter 1
The Storm

I was the only occupant of the large, four-bed hospital room in the Orthopaedic B ward when Dr Naomi Rahimi-Levene, my new haematologist, walked in. She looked at me warmly, saying she came about the results of the bone marrow biopsy and went straight to the point.

"You have multiple myeloma," she said, explaining it as a malignant, anti-immune blood disorder in the bone marrow that disables the immune system and destroys bone tissue. "There is no cure, but this kind of cancer is treatable," she continued, calmly outlining an initial treatment protocol that would last about eight months. I didn't ask many questions. Her voice floated above me. The words "cancer" . . . "incurable" . . . "treatable" . . . echoed repeatedly within me.

"So my back was killing me," I thought, as I remembered the last weeks of horrendous back pain that had brought me to the orthopaedic ward and this surprising diagnosis. As Dr Rahimi-Levene spoke, my mind drifted into flash-back mode to another reality 16 years earlier . . .

January 1991, Delray Beach, Florida

Just before the outbreak of the first Gulf War my mother called from South Florida saying, "I have bladder cancer. I will be operated on 16 January and I don't know how I can cope with this while worrying about you and the children in Israel. Can you come to Florida?" She probably would never have asked me to be with her if the prospects of war and Saddam Husain's threats to bomb Israel didn't scare her so.

"I'll be there with the kids if I can get four tickets," I immediately responded, knowing that if I were meant to be in the US, four tickets would be had. A few days later I found myself leaving work and taking my three children, Avital, Yael and Gadi, out of school for a flight to New York.

I knew there must be some deep purpose in what was happening. I had been actively on a spiritual path for about five years. I read avidly, meditated, practised tai chi and hosted a weekly meditation group in my home led by a woman who guided our meditations. I was just reading Dr Bernie Siegel's bestselling book, *Love, Medicine and Miracles*, about exceptional cancer patients and wanted to share his empowering message. What a coincidence. One woman in my meditation group suggested that I also take Louise Hay's now classic book, *You Can Heal Your Life*. I was not familiar with it, but trusted it would be important so I bought it in New York before boarding the plane to West Palm Beach. Finally, armed with optimism, a sense of purpose and two life-changing books, we arrived at my parents' home in South Florida, a day before Mom's operation.

After the operation the doctor informed my father and me that Mom's cancer was the most aggressive kind and had spread throughout her bladder. The protocol called for two six-treatment cycles of chemotherapy directly to her bladder. If the bladder was not 100 per cent clean and cancer-free after this, it would have to be removed, but my mother would live. My ears heard the words that described the situation, but my heart knew something else. I had never experienced this kind of "knowing" before. I clearly sensed that the doctor didn't believe the chemo would help her, he totally expected to remove her bladder and he thought she would live.

The doctor returned later when my mother was awake and repeated the same information to her. Again I sensed that other message. After the doctor left I looked at my mother and realized that on some level she had sensed it, too. I also perceived something that really shocked me.

"So you decided already," I said to my mother. She just looked at me, having no idea what I was talking about.

"So you decided already, huh?" I began again. "You decided that you are going to be an exemplary patient, go through all the chemotherapy sessions without complaining, because you are so brave and not a complainer, and then after two cycles of chemo treatments, you will not be 100 per cent cancer-free, so you will have your bladder removed and you'll live," I rambled. "Isn't that a waste?"

She looked at me blankly – nothing clicked.

I searched for a way to shake her up and said, "Mom, if I die tomorrow, you will live, but your quality of life will never be the same. Don't let your bladder go so easily.

Make another decision." Looking for something to challenge her mindset and clinch her understanding I said: "Decide that ONE series of chemotherapy will clean out your bladder 100 per cent. Make a different decision. Decide one chemo series will be enough. What have you got to lose?"

She looked at me and I saw something deep within her eyes change as she said, "OK."

When I told her I would help her every way I could, I saw and felt the new decision become her reality.

We read Dr Siegel's book together and worked on attitude, I guided her in meditation during her first chemo treatment and we investigated the source of her dis-ease using Louise Hay's directory in *You Can Heal Your Life*, which associates various parts of the body and *dis*-eases with mental attitudes and beliefs. I read Mom what Hay wrote about cancer: that it comes from "Deep hurt, longstanding resentments, deep secret or grief eating away at the self."[1]After those words left my mouth I thought, "Louise Hay really missed on this one. This isn't my mother at all." But when I turned to look I saw her sobbing. Out came a deep, dark, secret of childhood sexual abuse that had been secretly eating away at her for almost seven decades. This dark secret opened much to be healed.

I called a childhood friend, new age composer and musician Steven Halpern and told him about my mother's illness. He sent tapes of his healing music with subliminal healing messages. Mom played his music constantly, imagining that each ring of a bell turned cancer cells into healthy ones. We worked out a happiness diet, which meant trying to be surrounded with as many positive situations as possible to avoid tension and stress. I asked her to promise not to watch anything sadder than Walt Disney or Barbara Streisand on TV or in the movies. She took everything I could give her and developed her own visualization skills. After two weeks my kids and I returned to Israel and scud missiles. Mom and I remained in constant phone contact and continued to work together on attitude, healing, release and forgiveness.

Weeks later, while meditating, I wondered how she was doing. I saw myself inside a clear crystal cave.

When Mom called a few days later she said, "Guess what. I finished the first chemo series and my bladder is 100 per cent cancer-free. Can you believe it? My doctor doesn't.

He's so unsure and surprised that he's insisting on a second series of chemotherapy to be on the safe side."

Though the doctor didn't understand what happened, we both knew what she had done! I felt the power of the mind–body connection at work first hand. She did have the second series of chemo treatments "to be sure". From that day on my mom remained cancer-free and died in 2013 at the age of 91.

THE HEALING JOURNEY BEGINS

I heard myself say: "If I could guide Mom, I can guide me. If she could do it – so can I."

My haematologist was still talking . . .

I felt a connection to her, a trust. I felt her belief in the treatment she proposed. She said I would be given high doses of steroids immediately. Later that day I would be transported by ambulance to nearby Tel Hashomer Hospital to begin radiation treatments, which should significantly shrink the tumours in my spine and relieve the pain. The moment the doctor left the room, a lump welled up in my throat. The words "incurable"[2] . . . "treatable" . . . "CANCER" . . . exploded in my mind and I burst out crying. One of the most universally feared scenarios, being told that you have incurable cancer, had just become my reality.

And I cried. I cried my eyes out.

When the tears dried up, I was in an extreme new reality.

Some of the emotions that overwhelmed me were released with the tears and I felt clearer. From my experience with my mom, I knew decisions were being made, whether I was conscious of them or not. I had to become aware of my choices and not be steered by some automatic reaction like Mom almost was.

I took a few deep breaths to help me look at my feelings calmly. No, I didn't feel like I was going to die from this . . . but I really had no idea how I was going to live. I just hoped I would know somehow.

PRACTICES

Using self-inquiry to find the calm within your storm

As you've read in this chapter, being emotionally overwhelmed happens, especially in extreme situations. Since this state is not conducive to the practical consideration of options or decision-making, the first basic step is to quiet the emotional turmoil. Then you can use the following ideas and self-inquiry questions to focus on your own storm.

1. Release pent-up emotions, troublesome thoughts and nagging worries

- Crying, laughing or both together are great natural ways of letting go and creating a place for something new. So if you have the urge, don't hold back. Go for it. It's good for you. Actually laughing is so good that there is a form of yoga called "laughing yoga", which is fun, healthy and even available in many hospitals as well as through other venues.

- Another great way to release stress if you are physically able is through physical activity – e.g. the proverbial walk along the beach or in nature or a park, bicycling, swimming, running or even punching a pillow.

- And of course just breathing mindfully with your attention on each breath, can clear stress (see Part Two, page 144).

2. Think about the challenge ahead

Most people say they want to live, be healthy and pain-free. What's not to want? But my mom showed me there are unconscious influences like "playing the role of a good patient" and "fulfilling expectations" that are beyond our conscious awareness. In addition, being really sick has the benefit of being the centre of attention and caring. There are many unconscious facets to coping with illness of which we are not generally aware. Things must be clarified so the best decisions can be made. I invite you to think about cancer as an extreme challenge and ask yourself if you are ready to go to extremes to meet this challenge? Now can be the perfect time to pick up your journal or begin one and consider the following questions:

- Do you want to find ways to actively participate in your healing process to maximize your healing potential?

- Are you aware that many recent scientific studies show attitudes and proactive behaviours and activities can significantly empower healing potentials?

- What are your expectations? Take a few moments to jot them down. Since this book is about taking responsibility for your life, your health and maximizing your healing potential, try to be very honest with yourself.

- Where do you see yourself regarding your possibilities to heal?

  1. At the bottom
  2. Below average
  3. Average
  4. Above average
  5. At the very top

- If you like your thoughts, great; if not, you can always change them and your decisions, like my mom did.

3. Find quiet and stillness in the now

There are many options to enter stillness, so find one or more that work for you. Some people go into a state of quiet when they wash dishes, swim, go fishing or in the shower or a hot bath. Others meditate, practise yoga, qigong (pronounced "chi gong"), tai chi or a combination. Listening to meditation music or quiet background music can be very calming too. Each option facilitates a connection to the here and now, to being present, and from there into a zone of inner quiet. There is no correct option or correct way to meditate, and you will find more guidance on creating a meditation practice in Part Two (see page 153).

GUIDED MEDITATION 1 - CALM, LIGHT AND JOY

Use this guided imagery meditation to open your connection to the here and now and inner quiet. You may also combine parts of this meditation with other images that guide you to your safe space of tranquillity.

You'll find the text for this guided meditation in Chapter 21 (page 153) or listen to an audio recording at www.judyerel.com.

NOTES

1. Louise L. Hay, *You Can Heal Your Life*. Santa Monica, CA: Hay House Books, 1987; p. 159.
2. In-curable or "curable from within" according to Louise Hay, *ibid.*

Chapter 2
Linking Thoughts and Actions

My new reality was a big unknown. So I consciously decided to let my intuition guide me in the direction of what felt good and raised my spirits. I reached for a pen and notebook to journal in, and ideas began to flow. I know journaling helps me express my thoughts and focus on what action I need to take. I was glad I brought paper, pens and pencils to the hospital to "pass the time". For those who have never tried it, journaling is simply putting your thoughts on paper without filters or judgement by letting your hand rule your head and writing whatever comes into your mind . . . without censorship. When I'm finished I usually put the notebook away without even looking at what I've written. Sometimes I might take a look weeks later and sometimes not at all. The point is to express yourself, sometimes to get things off your chest, and sometimes to come to understanding and sometimes not. The result isn't important, the doing is.

It was time for a reality check, so I asked myself: "What do I think . . . no, what do I "know" can help me help myself?"

My answers were as follows:

- I trust in the mind–body unity that fostered Mom's exceptional recovery and I knew if my mother at 70 years old could do it, I was sure up for a try. After all, what did I have to lose?"

- I know that what you place your attention on influences how you experience the world – so somehow you get what you look for – be it the positive or the negative. When you look for good things, you find them. When you look for things to worry about, you surely find them too.

- I know that "what you consistently think about, expands" – for good and for bad. That means I should try my best to think about things that would place me in a positive direction.

- I know there is scientific proof of thoughts influencing biology and, for example, joyous thoughts enhance the immune system, while stressful thoughts suppress it. I had to become aware of my thoughts. You can't prevent negative thoughts from entering your mind, but you surely can decide how long you let them stay there.

- I know that Louise Hay's bestselling classic *You Can Heal Your Life*, would be one of my first resources to organize my actions. According to Louise Hay,[1] the back symbolically represents "the support of life".[2] Evidently something was seriously imbalanced in the way I've been supporting myself and perceiving my support system. Of course I know what I consciously want – I want to release all aspects of suffering and to support the aspects of joy, creativity, love, affluence, health and ease – more or less like most people. But that evidently was not how I lived my life or what I was experiencing. I was being seriously challenged.

- I know from my experience of meditating and focusing[3] that when you are just present with your attention on something like pain, its intensity can gradually lessen and even frequently disappears.

A few weeks earlier, as I was drawing alongside my art students in one of my private art classes, all I could think about was the excruciating pain in my back – so I drew it. I discovered by "chance" that drawing my pain was a wonderful and easy way to focus on it, be with it, "observe" it, "listen" to it and let it talk to me. I worked slowly. My hand reached for a pencil and a ruler and drew sharp triangles that reflected the sharp, burning pain. My paintbrush went to a box of watercolours and chose the blacks, hot reds and deep yellows – nature's warning colours. I worked intuitively – not thinking about what would come next. I expressed the pain in colours, lines and shapes and let it become something clearly separate from me. Immersed in drawing and painting, I entered another "zone",

one where I was not aware of time or pain. I was familiar with the joy and calm of creative expression, but I had never thought about or experienced its painkilling quality before. I was calm, but the drawing was not. The painting may have described what I felt, but as I painted I actually felt better, lighter. I worked very deliberately and slowly so it took several sessions to complete the drawing. (See Plate 1.)

I brought a sketchpad, pencils and pens to the hospital, even though the act of drawing had become more complicated – I learned that the cancer had collapsed a vertebra, which was the source of the excruciating pain. I was told to lie flat on my back (with only a 30-degree lift under my head) or wear a corset brace from collarbone to pelvis to protect my spine from the force of gravity. I lifted the upper bed to a 30-degree angle and rested my sketchbook on a beanbag lap tray on my raised knees. Again, I focused on the pain and again drawing it calmed me. Morphine was a great help too! Beginning a bit like a doodle, one line led to another. What I drew looked to me like animal-like entities scraping my spinal cord with sharp triangular shards resembling the pain from my first drawing. It looked like some sci-fi battle from *The Matrix*. When I drew it I wondered what it was all about. Now I knew. (See Figure 1 below.)

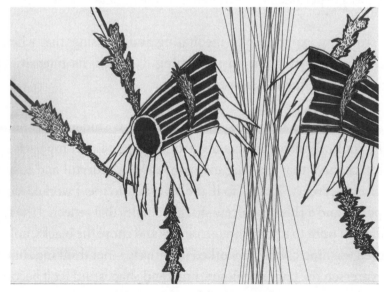

Figure 1: *Some of the Pain 2*, ink

Drawing, meditation and journaling became my basic tools to link thought and actions, and so create a new mindset. As an artist and art teacher I know the joy of drawing and painting and have seen enjoyment on hundreds of faces immersed in the simple act of creative expression. The very act of doing, creating has an importance that has nothing to do with the final product.

PRACTICES

Creative expression exercises to develop a healing mindset

Use the following inquiry questions and practices to explore your creative expression and develop your healing mindset.

1. What do you know/think can be of help to you at this time?

Take your journal and make a list of your own ideas on how to help yourself and/or use some of my ideas. Note ideas that may seem interesting, even if you are not sure they can help. It may be time to open up and try something new.

2. Colouring and/or drawing a mandala

Colouring a mandala[4] or sacred circle (in Sanskrit) is a wonderful, easy and very trendy creative activity that puts the doer in the quiet zone. You can use pens, pencils, coloured pencils, crayons or watercolours on paper, or whatever you like (see Chapter 23, page 178, for detailed instructions). You may choose an empty circle with no set design or one with a geometric design, or make up a design of your own with a compass and ruler. You can use the mandala formats provided below or find something on the Internet and then let yourself go. Even if you use the same mandala format again and again, each mandala you do will be different because you are at a different moment in time, with different feelings and sensations. If there is a particular feeling you want to express, take a moment to feel it, breathe deeply and then let your hand choose what it wants to use and where. You can fill the circle with colours, lines, shapes, objects and designs. There are no rules. Just let "your fingers work without thinking". That's what I consider working intuitively.

Remember, there are no wrong choices or mistakes. It's all part of your communication with your Self. If you want to express fear or pain, go for it. That's a great way of distancing the fear or pain from your inner being because you can look at it. You can even tear it up, burn it and/or throw it away to release these feelings. On the other hand you can just express what you feel at the moment without giving it a name. You do that by choosing each colour that catches your desire and placing it wherever you wish. You only stay within the lines if that's what you want. It is the doing that is most meaningful, because the creative act places you in a place, a zone that removes stress and lets the body renew itself gently. The best thing is that it's fun and simply feels good. Ideas and thoughts may pop into your mind while you are working. You can write them in the mandala or on the back of the paper, or not at all.

In the plate section (Plates 2, 3, 4 and 5), you can see mandalas coloured by people I've worked with, using pencils or watercolours. The first is a watercolour expressing burning pain (see Plate 2), the second expresses feelings about a difficult health situation (see Plate 3) and the third and fourth show the complex coping required by caregivers (see Plates 4 and 5).

Here are some mandala formats you can use (see Chapter 23, page 182, for step-by-step instructions for using a compass to draw the following geometrical mandalas).

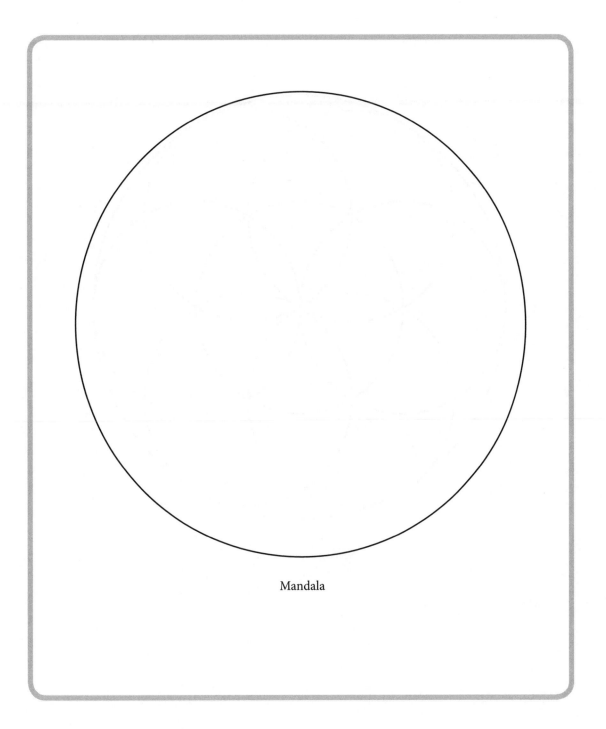

Mandala

Seed of Life Mandala

The Flower of Life Mandala

NOTES

1. Louise L. Hay is one of the founders of the self-help movement and author of many books, among them the *New York Times* bestseller *You Can Heal Your Life* with its famed list of different bodily ailments, their probable mental causes and new thought patterns to mentally heal one's body and one's life.

2. See Louise L. Hay, *Heal Your Body: The Mental Causes for Physical Illness and the Metaphysical Way to Overcome Them*. Carlsbad, CA: Hay House, 1982, p. 16.

3. Focusing is a method of communicating with one's body developed by Eugene Gendlin (*Focusing*. New York: Bantam Books, 1981, see also www.focusing.org) that I had learned several years ago by taking a course and reading a few books. Gendlin claims that sensed feelings, pain, discomfort are ways that the body is trying to communicate its needs. By providing feelings with space and having a dialogue with them, deep understanding can be gained and our realty is affected accordingly.

4. Mandala is the Sanskrit word meaning "sacred circle". It traditionally describes circular creations that begin at a centre point and radiate outwards, many times with symmetrical geometrical balance and symbolic meanings. Mandalas can be found in religious and secular carvings, paintings and drawings from prehistoric times to the present. Some varied examples can be seen in Indian painted mandalas, Tibetan sand mandalas, Native American sand paintings, ornamental stained glass rosette church windows, ancient circular formations like Stonehenge, labyrinths and sacred geometry. Jung considered the mandala the archetype symbol of the Self as well as the path to the Self, which he called individuation. He professed the therapeutic value of mandala drawings and their unification of opposites. Today drawing mandalas has become very popular, whether as free-flowing intuitive expressions, or with geometric forms and symmetry, as they are thought to promote communication with the unconscious, empowerment, balance and inner peace. I have been drawing and painting mandalas intuitively and with geometrical forms for almost two decades.

Chapter 3
Choice Is Where Power Lies

"We can't change reality, but we can change our attitude, thoughts and feelings about reality." To me this familiar saying implies that feeling you are a victim or being angry at the world or yourself or someone else is a choice, just as looking to maximize the positive potentials of treatment programmes is a choice.

I knew that choosing to see myself as a key force in my recovery and my health would demand an unwavering commitment. But what did that mean practically? I wasn't sure that I could always focus my thoughts, actions and feelings on the results I wanted? How could I be so sick and keep my ideas from being paralysed by the real physical suffering I was experiencing? How could I keep the thoughts of uncertainty, the why and what will be of it all, from eating away at my self-confidence?

Meditating taught me that I could disperse troublesome thoughts by practising mindful breathing,[1] but I would need more than that. How could I fill hours of "now moments" in a positive, meaningful way? What could I do when my now was really difficult? What was the most constructive way to focus on healing my illness and supporting the treatment options while in the midst of real physical suffering? And most important, if thoughts lead to experiences, what experiences did I want my thoughts to lead to?

For a start, I knew I wanted the best recovery possible . . . and with that thought I imagined becoming a statistical curve breaker. I saw myself as a smiley dot on the highest area of a healing chart, and I still wanted a life of joy, health, love and creativity. Since life is now, I decided consciously to fill each moment I could with as much joy, health, love and creativity as possible . . . minute by minute . . . I knew my life depended on it.

Clearly this was about more than how I handled this bout with cancer. This was about facing the fire-breathing dragon of paralysing fear that can leave us helpless, in denial or forgetful of the power of choice. This was about living my life to the extreme . . . about a possible path, an attitude, a decision to find the high road, no matter what – to live a life of joy and celebration now . . . in big things, little things, anything. Most of all, it was about finding a proactive way to touch the core of my mind–body intelligence – to connect me to me, to my power and compassion for myself and those around me. But how?

ON THE LOOKOUT

The feeling of empowerment that this insight and decision gave me was a beginning. I felt open, intensely attentive to my surroundings, my heart and myself. I decided to trust that life would show me answers to questions yet unrevealed.

I observed my thoughts and feelings: I felt protected; I trusted my doctors, the treatment proposed, and my path . . . so, I consciously decided that I was on a golden path that would take me to the best place possible, leaving the definition of that "place" open-ended and general. Thanks to opiate drugs my pain was being controlled, and I felt very energetic, extremely alert and curious from high doses of steroids.

I felt a level of active responsibility I had never known before. I left behind my usual optimistic, rose-coloured defence mechanisms and denial, and became conscious of my thoughts, feelings, actions and the energy they sent out into the world. Since I believe our external reality reflects an inner reality, I strove to articulate clear, specific and positively formulated thoughts that would be an emotional or energetic match to what I wanted to attract to my life. Like attracts like – that's the Law of Attraction.[2] Having no idea what the next moment would bring, I entered this new reality with my eyes wide open.

PRACTICES

Starting self-inquiry

The following self-inquiry exercise will help you to start thinking about what choices you are making by becoming aware of where you are placing your focus.

Take out your journal and note your responses to the following questions:

- If thoughts lead to experiences, what experiences do you want your thoughts to lead to?

- What have your thoughts been focused on?

- Do these thoughts make you happy? Do they place you in the direction you want to go? If not, what could you do or focus on to put you in the right direction?

- Are you ready to align your thoughts to the experiences you want to have? For example: a focus on critical and angry thoughts is not conducive to the desire to experience tranquillity, love or joy, whereas focusing on pleasing things is. The first step towards change is to become aware when your thoughts are not giving you good feelings. Pat yourself on the back each time you notice that critical, angry, frustrating thoughts have grabbed your attention. Try to let go of the thought and focus on something that brings you joy. If changing directions doesn't come easy I invite you to do something else entirely. For example, you might meditate, go for a walk, put your attention on something neutral, draw or paint that feeling/thought or colour a mandala (see Chapter 2, page 13) or even take a nap.

NOTES

1. Mindful – mindfully – filled with awareness, consciously, attentively, with intent. Mindful breathing is focusing your conscious attention on every moment of the in-breath, the out-breath and the space in between. When guiding meditations, I've always taught not to resist random distracting thoughts that may arise because that places our attention more firmly on the distraction. That's what's meant by "what you resist persists". It is enough to recognize the presence of the thought and then turn one's attention in the present moment back to the breath. That's how mindful breathing quiets mental noise.

2. For more about the Law of Attraction see www.Abraham-hicks.com and my short explanation in Appendix I (see page 188).

Chapter 4
Drama Turns to Adventure

A few hours after learning that I had cancer and deciding to find my way to meet this challenge, I found myself gazing at a cloud and treetop sky-scape through the windows of an ambulance. I was flat on my back, immersed in new perspectives as I was taken to Tel Hashomer Hospital for radiation treatments. I took out my notebook and a pen and started to observe my adventure.

Tuesday, 20 March 2007, Tel Hashomer Hospital
Marble lobby, colourful décor and decorations . . . I am wheeled on the ambulance stretcher bed into Tel Hashomer Hospital for my first radiation treatment. Many people are waiting for radiation – sick people. I realize I have not changed my definition of me . . . Careful with my words, I try to be positive, yet precise. I guess I can say, "I am challenged by a situation of imbalance that places me in a new experience . . . a new way of being. I am filled with acute awareness, new exactness."

Quiet. It is so quiet here. I am wheeled straight to the recovery room for special care. They carefully transfer me in the stretcher sheet to the hospital bed, keeping my back flat. The nurse opens a file for me as a patient in the oncology/radiation department. A doctor examines me, asks questions. I answer. A man sitting in another area of the room with an IV in his arm wears a knitted wool hat covering his totally bald head . . . A new camaraderie?

I feel myself letting go; accepting each moment . . . everything is a first . . . I am wheeled into the simulation room, transferred very gently in a sheet to the simulation bed, and measured for the radiation treatments. Everyone is very kind.

As I lie perfectly still, I hear my thoughts rhyme. I wonder who is in my head. "Whose words are these? Are they mine?"

I pray to create the best possible situation for myself and my healing.

Targeting vertebrae T6 through T10, a rectangle is drawn between my breasts in indelible ink to define the area to be irradiated. After several hours of measurements and calculations, I finally received a three-minute radiation treatment. I heard a buzzing noise but didn't feel a thing. My mind filled with the sound of rhyming words describing the light entering my body as purifying, clearing and clarifying. Could the steroids be talking? This was definitely not the process I was used to when I wrote poetry. I listened to the beautiful phrases in awe, sorry that I could not move to write them down. The sounds gave me the feeling that I wasn't alone; I felt protected and in the right direction. Since my decision to be on a golden path, I seemed to be on an extraordinary ride!

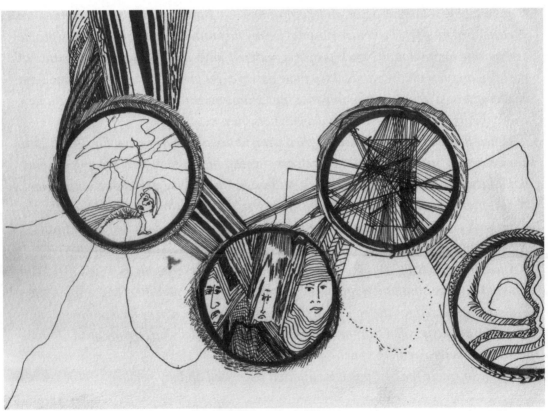

Figure 2: *Radiation Cleansing*, ink

Hours later, lying in my hospital bed, I reached for my sketchbook and the cup on the stand and intuitively drew four circles around it and let my pen doodle, filling in one circle at a time. These circles seemed like peepholes into the landscapes of my mind. I enjoyed doodling and tried not to impose artistic or sophisticated ideas. The circles filled from left to right, one by one and lines connected the circles. It looked like something was flowing into and through the circles. As I continued looking, I saw recognizable images and abstract shapes that challenged my understanding. (See Figure 2 above.)

Was this drawing graphically and physically expressing an intention to target memories, feelings and behaviour patterns held within my cells?[1] The first circle revealed an artist painting a ceiling in an unbalanced and probably painful position; the second had three sombre, anxious faces peeking through a tense, angular background. Lines pierced a rectangle in the third, while the last circle continued beyond the border of the paper with curving lines and more open space. Were the lines connecting the circles radiation rays that targeted the contents of each circle? Had I drawn the radiation rectangle, as a suffering artist, and the pain, anxiety and hardships that hopefully would choose to be released as the radiation flowed into and through the circles?

That night I couldn't sleep. My "usual feeling" of a poem wanting to be written nudged me as the phrase "sleep comes with difficulty" repeated itself until I reached for a pen and let the words flow onto the paper.

Sleep comes with difficulty.
Words awaken.
They come when eyes close.
They march across thoughts
Singing . . .
Whispering –
Create another way
To reach whole.
Deepen understanding and awareness;
Reveal an eloquent path of particles
Separating, re-joining, creating a new you,

A miniscule occurrence in the universe
Forming peace and love within.
Radiate below as above, above as below
All that is, is affected . . . one ray at a time.

A new world is being built within
And all around me.

Then I slept.

The next day the Professor, head of the orthopaedics surgery, came to see me. He said that he was sorry that it wasn't just mundane osteoporosis – but still, it wasn't catastrophic. He told me the radiation "would ease my pain, and that the best treatment for my vertebra was to do nothing". He said he was "hopeful" that the lesions[2] would recede and my back would be able to stabilize itself naturally. I would have to wear the corset brace for three to four months whenever I wasn't flat on my back (even in the shower or to go to the bathroom) and was told to refrain from bending, twisting my torso and, most important, I must not lift anything heavier than a glass of water.

I was taken aback by the simplicity of his treatment plan, especially since the first medical opinion I received had wanted to operate immediately. Feeling almost neglected, I asked him if this is what he would do if it were his back. He answered with an unequivocal "yes", explaining that since the pain was lessening and there was no neurological injury, an operation at this stage was at best uncalled for. There was always time for that. He was hoping that the radiation would shrink the tumours enough for my vertebra to stabilize itself.

I thanked my golden path and my eldest daughter for steering me to this doctor. I knew I would do everything I could to create optimum conditions for maximum healing. It was certainly worth a try.

Wednesday, 21 March 2007 – Radiation 2 Adventures
Radiation 2 was quick and to the point. I heard another poem in my head the whole time the radiation was working. It began: "From the first light of the Creator and the

first darkness – a new creation is in process filled with beauty and joy. The words then spoke of a new way of being – "a new paradigm", a process of combining and transforming what is, mobilizing inner strength and creating something new within me, within my body. Tears of joy welled up in my eyes and I felt blessed. I wasn't sure what the new paradigm was – but I was all for it.

Back in the hospital I reached for my sketchbook and pens and let my hands move where they liked. I was so limited in my ability to move, yet felt pulsing with life (and steroids).

I drew a circle around a cup – it became a head. I used pens of different widths to draw lines that became me– down to the sign of a broken rib I would only learn of a day later. (See Figure 3 below.)

Figure 3: *Static Dynamic Me*, ink

What I drew was one thing; the process of drawing was another. I drew each line slowly, aware of its uniqueness, imagining it drinking in life as I felt my heart open to everything I was feeling. For me the figure became filled with life and vitality, despite its static pose. I wasn't aware of time; I was in the zone beyond time . . . in the now.

The next day, on the ambulance ride back from my third radiation treatment, I scribbled part of the latest poem spoken in my head.

Dear one . . . floating through time
Dear one . . . floating through space
Your presence, flowing in all dimensions
Is part of the central sun.
The process you are has intentions
Rippling through all dimensions,
As you, and others at this time,
Embody a different possibility of being.

The words fell silent whenever the radiation machine stopped to change angles, and began again when the radiation started buzzing. I was fascinated though I wasn't sure what it meant. I felt alive; real time was now – I was curious and challenged. That was all I could remember from the dream-like, hugging presence that told me I wasn't alone and that what I was going through had purpose.

Later that day my dear friend Soufa, a shamanic artist, visited me in the hospital and I showed her my drawings.

"I see what you want to let go of," she said, "but what do you want to put in place of what is being radiated away?"

"Good question!" I thought for a moment. I liked the idea of deciding what I wanted to fill me with and replied, "Smiles."

"What does that mean for you?" She asked.

"I had a magical vacation a few years ago where everything went beyond any expectations I might have had or would have planned. I wondered what attracted so many wonderful experiences. You know, the law of attraction – like attracts like. If our life experiences reflect our inner world, I realized I must have been smiling at myself for the world to mirror such smiles back to me. I choose to be smiles inside and out."

After Soufa left I took a few quieting, deep breaths to centre myself and form a clear intention: to fill my cells, my vertebra, my being with what I needed to create the best recovery and the best life I could. I turned to a blank white page in my sketchbook. The black felt-tipped pen in my hand slowly began to leave its mark in the page's centre – the cell's centre, the vertebra centre, my centre . . . and worked its way outwards. My efforts became a mandala drawing with smiles and joy to fill each cell, my vertebrae and my whole being. (See Figure 4 below.)

Figure 4: *Filling My Self with Smiles*, ink

I was attentive to each millimetre, each line, each smile, face, heart, flower, dot and star as I drew. Whenever I looked at the drawing or showed it to someone, I was reminded of my choices and objectives . . . of how I wanted my insides to feel . . . how I wanted my life to feel. This totally positive drawing from the first stage of my treatments became one of the most influential expressions reflecting my mindset and a practical tool to meet cancer head on.

There was no further reason to remain hospitalized, so I was sent home to continue radiation treatments and follow-ups as an outpatient. The drawing was completed on the last day of my eight radiation treatments.

PRACTICES

Taking active responsibility

Taking responsibility begins with a decision and continues with focused, conscious actions. Consciously choosing and declaring what you want is an act of commitment to yourself. My intentions were very general at first. There was so much going on that the simple intentions of "reaching my maximum healing potential" and "filling myself with smiles and joy" seemed to say it all. They had a clear positive direction that did not encourage doubt or resistance and there was lots of room for pleasant surprises. I had entered a process where my decisions and intentions were guiding my focus and attention towards my goals.

Now it's your turn.

1. Self-inquiry

I invite you to take your journal and write down one or more decisions or intentions as concisely and positively as you can. Focus on what you want in a positive way – no negatives. Keep it simple and general. Some other examples are "I intend to maximize my healing potential", "I see myself on a wonderful path to recovery" and "Each cell in my body is opening to its greatest wellbeing, balance and harmony."

2. Nonverbal activity – creative, physical and practical

There are many nonverbal activities that can be used to express intentions. Since making art is my mode of nonverbal creation, most of my examples and instructions are related to these personal interests and strengths. Drawing is just one creative way that is certainly easily accessible to most people, with inexpensive and readily available supplies that can be used at home or in a hospital. Making or not making this choice should not be based on feelings about artistic ability. The quality of your work, in this, or any modality, isn't important. The process of doing it is. Do you have a creative activity preference? Anything you feel comfortable with and enjoy doing is a good place to start. You can express yourself through the visual arts of drawing or painting, making collages, photography, sculpting with clay, play-dough or even mashed potatoes. You can nonverbally create in the field of the performing arts that focuses on playing music, singing, dancing or acting out what you want to create, or even create a video. You may consider physical activities like running, walking, yoga or qigong more to your liking to express your intentions and fill yourself with positive qi/prana/good energy. Or you may like making practical objects to express intentions through carpentry, cooking, baking, weaving, embroidering, patchwork, or quilting – or anything else you can think of. Just enjoy the doing.

3. Nonverbal challenge – what do you want inside you?

Now I invite you to try a nonverbal creative exercise to express your intentions. The aim is to express your intentions and feelings through the creative action of your choice. Nonverbal creative expression, like meditation, takes place in the here and now of the right brain and quiets inner chatter.

- Take a full breath, sense your intention – what you want to have inside you – and then begin. If you are drawing, for example, intuitively begin to doodle, colour or draw freely. Let the lines, shapes and colours flow.

- Work intuitively. Let your hands, body and heart speak through how and what they create. There is no need to plan or know what the result should be ahead of time. Rules don't count . . . fun does.

- The most important thing is to let your inner voice of guidance have a safe platform for expression with no judgement or criticism – the doing is important, not the artistic result.

GUIDED MEDITATION 2 - UNITING WITH INTENTIONS

Before using this meditation, take some time to formulate your intentions for healing and then be sure to keep them in mind during your practice.

You'll find the text for this guided meditation in Chapter 21 (page 155) or listen to an audio recording at www.judyerel.com.

NOTES

1. In *Quantum Healing: Exploring the Frontiers of Mind/Body Medicine* (New York: Bantam Books, 1989), Deepak Chopra, the renowned endocrinologist and author, speaks of the interactive mind–body connection. He asserts that all that we are becomes part of our mind–body intelligence and that all these memories exist at the cellular level.

2. Pathological changes in the bone tissue.

Chapter 5
A New Challenge: Ordinary

On the way home, after stopping for some cash at an ATM, my daughter Avital suggested we cross the street for some real coffee at Cup O' Joe's. When the server came with two mugs of latté and a selection of freshly baked cookies, tears filled my eyes and flowed conspicuously down my face. I was embarrassed by being so overwhelmed. I couldn't believe that I could sit there like a "regular" person, enjoying coffee, talking, listening . . . so ordinary, so commonplace, and now so remarkably exceptional.

Home was another matter. I live alone, but could no longer be alone. I couldn't pour myself a cup of coffee or tea, dress myself, reach my feet when taking a shower or lift my hairdryer, let alone prepare my meals. If my glasses fell, I couldn't bend down to pick them up. I was heavily medicated with narcotic painkillers (thank goodness), stuffed with steroids, plus anti-this's and anti-thats. I needed full-time nursing care and help through the bureaucratic mire that employing a caregiver entails, which meant filling pages and pages of forms for my health provider, national insurance and who knows what else. You have to be healthy, with your wits sharp and focused, to do all that.

My golden path continued as my Avital gracefully helped me through it all. I was in daily contact with the rest of my immediate family living in the USA – daughter Yael, son Gadi and my sister and mother. I did my best to focus on the love and support that appeared from all directions and decided that the universe and life was doing its best for me.

I rented a hospital bed and placed it in my living room, creating a new environment with a new status. The living room became a light and spacious day room, opening into my small garden. We found a wonderful caregiver, Carolina. My family, friends and neighbours were there for me. I was overwhelmed with waves of gratitude.

Each day a different friend drove me to the hospital for the remaining five radiation treatments. Oxycontin and oxycodone helped me manage the pain. I had the car seat in maximum recline and, though the ride was difficult, I actually looked forward to the treatments. Not only were they helping my back, I had my own private poetry readings in my head. The poems began with the buzz of radiation and fell silent when the machinery moved to change angles. The words played with me, as if to say that its flow wasn't under my control. I remained still, enjoying.

One night, words inside my head nudged me to pick up the pen and paper that were always close by:

A short message, dear one, before your eyes close into rest . . .
This is one of the best experiences of your life – joining reality and intention,
Creating a suspension of judgement and an opening of your wingspan.
You are a new health situation – a challenge to your life and to all around you.
Bless you for the courage and optimism that create an out-of-the-box experience.

Yes, sink into a new awareness of your body,
Feelings of photon bombardments – steroids vibrating throughout.
Build a new spine with light cement – woven into old bone
Healed naturally.

As for pictures of bones, your bone –
Paint it . . . healed and at normal size.
Use printouts of x-rays – rice paper, gold leaf.

How do you create a healthy back?
What is a healthy back?
How do you measure health? In pain, x-rays, function???

I realized I was guiding myself or being guided to heal my back using visualizations of light cement and create a series of drawings from concrete images of my bones in order to heal them. This meant defining my goals in practical detail. I was in awe. Good thing I wrote it down.

GOLDEN PATH QUEEN . . .

I needed help with everything. What "gift meaning" could I find in this? I began to think about my extreme neediness and dependence, what it meant to receive and how I received. Was I comfortable receiving so massively? Sure, I liked being served and enjoyed attention, but not total dependence or pity. On the other hand receiving can also have meaning when you enable others the opportunity to give . . . and sometimes that means having to ask for what you lack. Feeling lack is a part of me that I have great difficulty looking at . . . as if being in lack is evidence of failure, something to be terribly ashamed of. Where are the good choices here, I wondered? If you receive out of lack, as someone with no choices or resources, wouldn't everything received be coloured in some shade of victimhood, shame or self-pity? I knew I could easily fall into that pattern, but that was not what I wanted! I wanted the complete opposite, which would be? To receive like a queen, out of grand entitlement, tinting everything in royal celebration and joy. And because members of a royal court surrounded queens, I would assume that those around were definitely not miserable, manipulated victims either. I now had a Philippine Princess in charge of the palace and loving members of court tying to make my life easier.

I was conscious of doing my best to focus on the good that was happening. That was easy to say and want but sometimes my extreme dependence, magnified by the serious psychological and emotional side effects of the steroid medications, resulted in the behaviour of an irrational control freak that I call my "shadow queen".

My optimism wasn't always easy for those around me, either. I sensed they feared I was either back in my deep denial mode with Pollyanna, rose-coloured glasses glued in front of my eyes, or worse, high on the morphine derivatives I was taking. I claimed I was just trying to be in the now – consciously maximizing joy and minimizing fear in each moment in order to create the moments to come. What was reality? I really don't know – I just kept trying to live "like attracts like" in an unlikable situation.

My old yardstick of how days are filled didn't work anymore. There was little I could or had to do. There were still 24 hours in a day, every day. Some days were easy to fill, others less – each day was the same, but different.

There were times when I cried a lot, overextended myself, missed my mommy, and wanted someone to kiss my booboo and tell me everything would be OK in the morning. Many times I felt fragile, like any little pressure could break me apart, causing my bones to crumble. And there were times I was in clear focus, creating order in my life and setting goals.

And I journaled:

The whole house went through Carolina's spring cleaning "radiation treatment". The house glows from walls scrubbed with soapy scotch bright, floor panels cleaned by a toothbrush, closets taken apart, nothing escaped. All the dirt, all the heavy energy that had touched this house in the past has been cleansed in every room, closet, nook and cranny. I am amazed at the synchronicity of the irradiation of my inside and outside environments.

The house is filled with flowers and colours. Am I?

Sometimes I vented and whined in self-pity . . . finding a way to accept even that part of myself as seen in the excerpt below:

I am beginning to face how ill I am . . . How much care and being cared for I require. I cry at how stupidly hard I have been on myself – how blind to me and my needs and my hurts.

And sometimes I was able to look at myself from a more distant perspective.

I cry easily – with joy, with gratitude, in sadness. The intensity and swings of my moods seem beyond my control – a known side effect of the dexamethasone steroids, which can make you crazy and even psychotic. Oh my, this is going to be interesting indeed.

Breaking news: Yael and Gadi (my children living in the USA) will be coming over the next months to be with me and share the burden of a sick parent that has fallen all on Avital so far.

Chemo starts next week.

PRACTICES

Journaling to gain insight

As I mentioned in an earlier chapter, observing your reality and feelings through journaling can be invaluable to the healing process. I invite you to try even if you are not used to writing. It can help you view and express your reality at a given moment in time without letting one moment evaporate into the next.

I began on individual sheets of paper, but found it more convenient to use a journal or simple notebook that kept everything in one place. You can see additional perspectives while writing or when you look at what you wrote at a later "now" time.

So here's how to start and what to do if you're new to journaling:

- Take a pen or pencil and write down your thoughts.

- Let your hand rule your head and write whatever comes into your mind . . . without censorship. You might even write, "I can't think of anything to write" again and again until a thought comes through your pen.

- You may journal about experiences that are happening, reflect upon what is around you or jot down thoughts that pop into your mind.

- When you're finished, put the notebook away without even looking at what you wrote. You can look later or not at all. The point is to express yourself, to get things off your chest.

- You may come to new understandings or not. Again, the result isn't important, the doing is.

Chapter 6
A Labour of Empowerment

Before giving birth for the first time, I was happy and excited, even though I knew childbirth isn't considered to be a picnic. Now before chemo I felt something curiously similar. I saw myself in the process of giving birth to my healthy self and wanted this to be a labour of empowerment. If I was to get the maximum benefit from the treatment – there was work to be done. I had some extreme training to do. As I reached for a pen and paper questions and words began to flow. What came out was an uncensored brainstormed monologue of thoughts, feelings and questions.

- *What is the source of this cancer? What's "the deep dark secret or deep hate, hurt or resentment" that Louise Hay describes that is behind my reality of cancer?*
- *How will I look with a bald head?* ☹
- *What insights can I gather before chemo?*

I reminded myself:

- *Paint/draw healed bones.*
- *Don't fight reality. Byron Katie[1] says arguing with reality is the source of suffering. Be on the lookout for ways to accept and love this reality. Everything depends on perception, subjective perception.*

Then I remembered a process Soufa mentioned a few months earlier, which involved releasing what you no longer want in your life and supporting all that you want to flourish. Reminiscent of spring cleaning, it was time to let go of the old and out-dated to make room for the new and relevant. I continued:

- *Make a list of qualities, behaviour patterns and situations that I consciously choose to release from my life.*

- *Make a list of the qualities, behaviour patterns and situations that I want to nurture and thrive in me and in my life.*
- *Perhaps the chemo will wipe out the relevant cell memories from all my cells? Can I intend for the chemo to release the memories and feelings? Can I choose/ intend to clean what I want along with the cancer cells? Maybe . . . why not?* ☺
- *I could talk to my cells through guided imagery: I'll prepare my body to forgo resistance and open to its natural healing power. I'll try to unite my mind and body with the healing power of smiles to myself.*
- *The days ahead may reveal difficult side effects from the treatments* ☹ *or . . . they may not* ☺ *. . .*

1968, Boston, summer before my senior year at Cornell University
I was hospitalized, diagnosed with a life-threatening, non-cancerous blood condition that required extremely high doses of prednisone steroids and the doctor was dutifully informing me of the "side effects that may occur". I listened to the words "moon face" and "weight gain" and thought mischievously, "He said 'may occur', not would occur! No way! I'm 20 years old – moon-face and weight gain are totally unacceptable!"

Then he said, "stomach ulcers" and I thought, "Got it covered. Dad had ulcers so I know what an ulcer diet is – I'll put myself on an ulcer diet as a precaution . . . and nothing will happen." Then he said "facial hair" and I thought "Oh shit!"

That year I lost weight, looked fabulous, my stomach was fine and five little hairs grew under my chin.

SMILING INTO THE PRESENT

I made a deal with myself right then and there to have the minimum side effects from the chemotherapy that my body could agree to. I sensed it was important not to commit to a specific result and perhaps subconsciously test myself. I remained detached from the outcome as I attached myself to the process. Then I decided not to be afraid because, after all:

I am always in the right place at the right time . . . and guided to my highest and greatest good.

On one of Soufa's visits she suggested that I draw my cancer cells and my healthy cells and then burn the sick cells and plant the healthy ones. That was a good way to anchor thoughts in action. I did the drawing with joy, but the artist in me couldn't destroy them. Instead, on the back of the page I declared in ink that the cancer cells were dead and gone and the healthy cells spread and blossomed throughout the earth of my body.

I drew the healthy cells based on crystal forms of water as shown in Dr Masaru Emoto's *New York Times* bestselling book, *The Hidden Messages in Water*[2] that I had recently read. His scientific experiments showed that the physical form of water crystals reacted positively and negatively to words in all languages. Words or thought forms[3] of approval, gratitude, love and support generate whole, symmetrical crystals and words of disapproval and humiliation create broken, distorted crystals. Since our body is 70 per cent water and water reacts to thoughts and words, I drew these mandala forms joyfully filling myself with a sense of health. On the other side of the paper I drew the cancer cells all bunched together, misshapen and intruding on each other. (See Figure 5 opposite.)

Without planning, I supplemented the visual with verbal descriptions of the qualities of the two different groups. I tried not to hold anything back. Healthy cells were conceived as centred, defined, having clear boundaries, knowing who they are, having clear intentions, being creative, balanced, containing pure water that forms crystals of love, gratitude, life, joy, unity, beauty, purity, health, laughter and smiles. I see these as the qualities that I want in the healthy me, along with a strong, resilient immune system. The cancer cells are described as disharmonious, aggressive, invaders and victims. They are characterized by wild growth, and an impinging, unorganized, out-of-balanced nature. They are off-centre, lost in insecurities, with cloudy, unclear boundaries and unsure intentions. They are critical, ugly, lacking, fearful, self-deprecating, sloppy, painful, self-destructive, angry, hostile, and feel lost and guilty. I was reiterating and re-clarifying what weakened my immune system and needed to be released and what strengthened my immune system and needed to be nurtured. I looked at my drawing and read the words over and over to absorb their essence into mine.

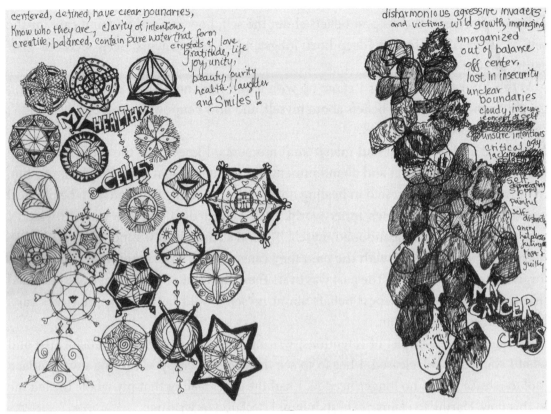

Figure 5: *My Healthy Cells – My Cancer Cells*, ink

SPENDING THE DAY WITH LOUISE, MONDAY, 9 APRIL 2007

I took out my copy of Louise Hay's *Heal Your Body* and, to clarify things to myself, copied her chart format, listing only the physical problems I was experiencing. Next to each problem I copied her list of probable mental causes and the new thought patterns for creating change. I wrote, read and reread, letting the ideas sink in, sensing what seemed to fit and what didn't. I tried to see the larger picture that was forming. Relevant issues for me revolved around: bones, bone marrow, blood disorders, cancer, the back, T8 vertebra, pain, tears. For example, I have cancer in the bone marrow. She writes that the bone marrow "represents the deepest beliefs about the self, how you support and care for the self".[4] Cancer comes from a "deep hurt, longstanding resentments, deep secret or grief eating away at the self . . . "[5]

When I put them together I came up with a question: how did I let a deep hurt and grief influence my deepest beliefs about myself, and how I supported and cared (or didn't care) for my essence, my core?

I looked at the lists and had many "aha" moments. I knew that the profoundly deep hurt of infidelity, betrayal and abandonment was the emotional core of my cancer, but, to be truthful, I was interested in healing not blaming. If I truly believed that the physical world is a reflection of one's inner world, then I needed to face the ways in which I rejected, betrayed, and abandoned myself. To heal such a deep wound, I knew I had to release the patterns along with the pain they caused. And, most important, I needed to forgive – especially myself. The past was over. The only point of power was now. I decided that from now on my deepest beliefs about myself would faithfully support my care, health and self-appreciation.

So again I created a list of intentions, writing what I wanted to be transformed and what I wanted to be released. I began to see the chemotherapy as serving my agenda: a tool to release what I no longer needed. I had the quiet feeling that my whole life led me to this now. Daring to claim my best dream, I declared in writing:

I focus my beliefs on total wellbeing – on joy, trust, acceptance and self-love, as the joyous creator/artist paradigm becomes the basis of my creativity, my expression and my life.

Cancer cells leave my physical, mental and energetic being – never to return. Great joy and gratitude celebrate this transformation process. My soul energy and the cells of my physical body unify in joy. Healthy and transformed cells remain part of me and those cells that leave for elsewhere, never to return, are thanked for their participation in my journey. This transformation creates the continuous opportunity to create a free flow of joy in my life. My bones support me well. The universe reflects my caring and supports my greatest good. With the joyous expression of my life comes clarity.

When I wrote the words on paper, thoughts became action; the words became a prayer, a command to be reread over and over with deep intent. In short, I visualized the best I could think of – and dared to believe. What did I have to lose?

MORE PREPARATION FOR CHEMOTHERAPY

Although it was almost 17 years since I had read Bernie Siegel's book *Love, Miracles and Medicine*, I vividly remembered that attitude towards treatment correlated highly with the treatment's effectiveness and minimized side effects. But how do you create a positive attitude towards chemotherapy, something so unknown, scary and notorious? The catchy phrase, "what you resist persists" came to mind and I felt its relevance. Maybe if I accepted the chemo with detachment, or even beckoned it into my cells to do its magic and then imagined it washing out of me without resistance, I would receive its benefits with minimum negative aspects.

I looked at the word "chemotherapy" as I wrote it on the computer and the word "mother" jumped out at me. As I separated the syllables I said out loud: "Che-mother-apy", I realized that "apy" is a suffix for therapy, "che" sounds like "chi", as in energy (like in tai chi), and "mother" – well, she loves me. She does the best she can – be it my mother or Mother Earth or Mother Nature, and motherhood is the most powerful force of nurturance. So here I am about to have mother energy therapy. "OK . . . That makes it a bit more palatable."

Chemo is meant to clean out rogue cells and I thought that was a great idea. But why stop there? I wanted it to clear away the need and energy that created these cells, too. Was that possible? I didn't know, but since the thought had entered my mind, perhaps on some level it was. In his book *Quantum Healing*, Deepak Chopra says that, although cancer may be in one area of the body, the other cells of the body "know" and are affected by the sickness and the treatment. Each cell contains cellular memories of the whole. I wanted to release everything in my entire body's cellular memory that was related to not being true to my essence and not caring for myself properly.

I kept on with this monologue/dialogue between me and myself. What did I need to release at the cellular level? I looked over the list of qualities and behaviour patterns I wanted the mother energy therapy to help me purge from my life. I also had insights from drawings of my healthy cells and my cancer cells, which boasted a tight verbal description. I felt energized and empowered instead of helpless and weary. I smiled, feeling myself in a win-win situation. But along with the list of all that I wanted to leave my body, I had another thought:

What if the butterfly effect is true?

If we really are all part of one interconnected whole, then everyone and everything has an influence on everyone and everything else. That's the idea behind the effect a butterfly flapping its wings in Southeast Asia has on the weather in Northern Canada. If everything can be reduced to energy and energy has no boundaries, then reality becomes a hall of mirrors where at some level, everything reflects everything and affects everything. My reality reflects and affects my input back at me, along with the input of everyone else, back at me, back at them and so on and so on.

Then I thought about other people's thoughts and the effect they may have on me. Israel is a small country where news travels fast. More and more people knew that I had cancer, a collapsed vertebra, around-the-clock nursing care and who knows what else. I considered all the worried, fearful thoughts and pessimistic exaggerations that were energetically coming in my direction? I had to do something. I didn't want thoughts of "Oh my G*d, did you hear Judy has cancer in her blood and bones, her back is broken and she was so spiritual or whatever." No, this wouldn't do. I had to make every part of my environment work for me and with me.

Was I being given an opportunity to create a support system to suit my worldview? My ideas were very clear to me now and I was going to make my butterfly wings count. I was searching for that new paradigm and knew it began here and now.

Defining the problem helped create the answer. I knew what I wanted and what I didn't want. I wanted smiles, like those I filled my body with during the radiation. That's what I wanted to create in place of the dis-ease. I also wanted good thoughts, positive thoughts, healing thoughts, fun and joyous thoughts surrounding me. And then it came to me – email (Facebook, YouTube and Twitter were just in their infancy). I would invite everyone and their cousins to an international celebration – a virtual party – friends, family, acquaintances, students, teachers from my school, friends from my hiking study group, translation colleagues and clients, my doctors, nurses, everyone – spiritual, non-spiritual, religious and non-religious, Jewish, non-Jewish, optimists and pessimists and other-ists alike. Email invitations to a virtual farewell party were sent to people in two languages on four continents and I invited them to invite their friends – the more the merrier. I would create my mirror and let everyone look straight at it and reflect it back to me. At the same time, I would open another way to win-win with transparency, clarity and joy. And so my virtual farewell celebrations were born with a wink and giggle.

Subject: Update and invitation to a virtual party (English)
To: Everyone on my mailing list
Sent: Tuesday, 10 April 2007 11.17 a.m.

Hi,
I am starting my first chemotherapy procedure tomorrow, Wednesday, April 11. This is the next step in the process transforming the essence of my bone marrow from diseased to totally healthy. According to Louise Hay, bone marrow represents the deepest beliefs about the self and how one cares and supports one's self, so I choose to see this as a wonderful opportunity for me to open myself to all the wonderful things I know I deserve. To name a few, I choose to see myself in total wellbeing, with joy, love, flowing creativity, perfect health and lots of money. So even though I will be hospitalized for four to five days at Assaf Harofe Hospital with continuous, slow-drip intravenous chemotherapy that targets the cancerous cells throughout my bone marrow. And though I don't really know what to expect – it also sounds like a great reason for a celebration . . . no?
So I wish to invite you to my first virtual farewell party, bidding farewell to the cancer cells in my bone marrow as they leave my body, aura, and energy forever!
I have decided that these cancer cells don't suit my life or creativity anymore. They contain all that is not love – all that is connected to disharmony, wild growth, victimhood, lack, doubt and the suffering artist/creator. They contain pain, fear, anger, sorrow, hardship, criticism, self-destruction, self-denial. These distorted cells have lost their inner beauty

and centre and no longer reflect my Self. They are appreciated for any good that they may have brought my way, but are thanked doubly for moving out of my body and aura – never, ever to return.

You are invited to virtually celebrate, aid and support my farewells.

How to participate in my virtual farewell party? Just use your imagination – even for a moment, any time between Wednesday and Sunday. Imagine, pray, send a thought, love, light. Imagine me happy, bidding farewell to these cancer cells (using my soul powers with the help of the chemotherapy), thanking them for the part they played in my life and seeing them leave my body and aura forever.

Let's clink glasses of virtual red wine! I have a great virtual caterer and there will be the virtual music of your choice, all in pleasant surroundings and happy colours, I'll be dressed in the very flattering hot pink, polka-dot Assaf Harofe Hospital pyjamas.

Please invite any loving friends to my party too.

I thank you for being part of my life.

Lots of love,

Judy

Then I clicked "send" . . . and smiled. It was time for chemo and I was ready.

PRACTICES

Che-mother-apy preparation review

Here is a recap of the key points for preparing your mind and body for chemotherapy. Relate to what feels right for you. Practise using your intuition and let one thing lead to another. Know that whatever you do is right for you simply because you do it.

- **Brainstorm and jot down ideas:** You may want to include some ideas that I brainstormed and continue on your own or just note things to do, fears, feelings, questions, relevant memories and ideas that pop up in your head. Try not to hold back. These ideas can guide you on your intuitive path to your greatest good.

- **Demystify the fire-breathing dragon of chemotherapy:** If you are having or need to have chemo or biological therapy, try to find ways to accept it. Imagine it as a great helper. Visualize that you let go of it and it lets go of you with ease after it does its magic. Fear creates resistance and that just holds things in place. And remember, che-mother-apy can be viewed as mother energy therapy and biotherapy can be thought of as therapy of life because bio = life.

- **Enjoy the process:** The more I prepared myself, the greater my sense of empowerment. Acknowledge your enjoyment and empowered feelings. Expressing gratitude is one way of many and it is very powerful energy.

- **Use creative expression to increase clarity and enjoyment:** I invite you to draw healthy cells and cancerous cells, or use words, music or any language to describe your feelings and understandings of the differences. Touching deep feelings helped me clarify my understandings and my desires.

- **Release any unwanted, unnecessary, and out-dated patterns, situations and behaviours to make room for something new and more suitable:** You can start by creating order and reorganizing in your external environment, for example: something in your house, your desk, your room. You can even imagine that you are ridding yourself of the unwanted within as you wash dishes cleaning away the remains on a dirty plate, etc.

- **Form clear intentions:** Brainstorm lists (see above), ideas and hunches can be used to stimulate more ideas and to help form clear intentions. Remember to use positive language to intend what you want.

- **Take care of your environment:** Be conscious of everything you are absorbing from friends or reading materials so make sure it is compatible with your chosen path. For example, I stopped Googling after a search led me to very pessimistic information about multiple myeloma and a prognosis of a very short life. Since I decide what I believe, I could have chosen to make the Internet information my reality; after all, it was written in black and white. But I didn't, because it did not echo what I sensed from my doctor or myself, nor was a dismal short future harmonious with my idea of a golden path. (A year later I learned that the dismal material was true several years ago, but now quite inaccurate and not up to date.)

- **Consolidate support:** This of course is a very personal thing. I decided to go so public because my illness was so visible to anyone that saw me. I found that going public with emails that stated my ideas, decisions and commitment to myself had an extremely empowering effect on me. I could really feel myself fill up with determination. I hoped that inviting others to support the clear statements of my intentions would create a flow of positive energy to nurture my best dream scenario and a win-win situation. On the other hand, sometimes it is better to keep things private. There may be many reasons for this. Think about why. If it is because you don't want to trouble even the people closest to you, perhaps you should reflect on how much support you think you deserve. If you decide to only tell a close few because you don't want to fall into the trap of feeding off self-pity and attention for being sick . . . you can reflect on that too. I did. Recently I had a small, cancerous growth in my breast and had surgery and radiation. This time I only opened myself to close family, close friends and those who could give me information. I didn't hide it, I just didn't mention it. I knew I could fall too easily into a trap of enjoying the attention received for being sick.

NOTES

1. See *Loving What Is*, in which Byron Katie, the author and founder of "The Work" (http://thework.com/en/do-work), leads the reader to understand what "inquiry" is all about and that all suffering comes from arguing with reality.
2. Also featured in the movie *What the Bleep Do We Know*, found on YouTube.
3. Dr Emoto considers words to be thought forms. He demonstrates that the similar meanings in different languages create similar kinds of crystals that can be differentiated from other meanings or thought forms.
4. See Louise Hay, *Heal Your Body*, p. 20.
5. *Ibid.*, p. 22.

Chapter 7
Seven Days of Moments

Most chemotherapy is given in outpatient care, for a few hours; however, my particular protocol called for 96 net hours of hospitalized chemo. I entered an extreme chemotherapy journey as if I were touring a strange land. It started with a visit to my haematologist, Dr Naomi Rachimi-Levene, where I had my blood tested and received explanations about everything I could think of. Then it was off to the ward I would eventually think of as my hospital home. I journaled to help me note, notice and observe. Sometimes I searched for insights and sometimes just to witness meditations and visualizations. Words and drawings reflected where my thoughts and my focus went. Here are some selections from April 2007.

Day one

Before the chemotherapy began an intravenous port needed to be placed into the large vein at the top of my thigh as an entranceway for the chemo. The doctor underestimated my body's super sensitivity and did not find the entrance point on the first few tries. I needed and was given more anaesthetics but I was beginning to panic. I told myself to breathe deeply, trying to connect to an inner calm I couldn't hold on to. I placed my focus on my breath, breathing mindfully from one moment into the next . . . and the next . . . each breath held on to the next . . . I wasn't sure how long I was doing this or could continue. I thought I would lose it and scream but I kept focusing on breathing – and then all of a sudden it was over. The procedure ended and was no longer my present, thus no longer a problem.

It begins . . .

When the first of four 24-hour drip bags of chemotherapy was connected, I was overwhelmed by its striking translucent coppery colour. A luminous red gold flowed into my veins and opened my heart to the che-mother-apy that would create great changes in my body. I found something unexpected to really love about it – its colour!

Day two

My shaman friend, Soufa, had suggested I draw two self-portraits – "me and my disease" and "me and my recovery". By now I knew I wouldn't burn or bury them as instructed, but I drew. Most of the day I focused on "me and my dis-ease"; I drew lying down with a slight rise under my head while leaning the paper on the beanbag lap tray that rested on my raised knees. I let myself play around in pencil until I found what I wanted and then I went over the lines in ink. I tried my best to find a free and unconstrained expression of my suffering, without beautification. Knowing there would be another drawing, the healed me, gave me the freedom to be honest with myself. I was surprised and pleased that my lines were articulate beyond words. (See Figure 6 below.)

The T8 vertebra was speared; stabbed in the back; the torso resembled a big bone and the background of pain spikes and cell textures added tension and stress. I tried to

Figure 6: *Me and My Dis-ease*, ink

Figure 7: My sketch of Picasso's *Woman Ironing*, pencil

capture some of the shoulder's heaviness found in Picasso's *Woman Ironing* (see Figure 7 above), which I have loved since I first saw it in the Guggenheim collection in New York when I was a young girl. But my hands looked like paws dragging the body forward; I guess I felt like a wounded animal. I drew for hours and then, since I created a virtual party, I figured it was time to attend. I journaled.

Sitting in a wonderful calm at my virtual farewell party, I visualize myself saying goodbye to the cancer cells and all that is not love as they leave the party and my body. I'm feeling calm, safe, healthy and loved. All is well.

Writing and drawing focused me in the present and being present in my imagination seemed more real than the hospital room I was in. Later the calm disappeared. I was having problems with my cell phone. I felt totally isolated, alone and lost on an emotional rollercoaster of frustration.

My phone isn't working and the replacement still doesn't work. I want to scream. I actually cry. I want to jump off a roof and just die, really not exist anymore . . . and over such nonsense. I feel crazed and it doesn't help to know that this is a known side effect of the medication I take. I feel like I lost all boundaries and control over myself, like a two year old in a temper tantrum. Finally I take up a pen and my sketchbook and try to put the explosiveness of the dexamethasone into lines, into order, into boundaries. (See Figure 8 below.)

When I finished the drawing, I felt calmer, something opened, relaxed. I could breathe. The effect of the drawing process amazes me – it changes my reality.

Figure 8: *Dexa Lines*, ink

Day three

I slept and feel rested. My telephone was replaced but the phonebook was lost. Some people are gone from my life, yet, a sense of calm has returned.

In the wee hours – my here and now: calm, I am content, on purpose I write to document this amazing process . . . perhaps this will turn into a book? I listen to my body for signs of comfort and discomfort. I have a heightened sense of honouring all – each thing I feel – blessing it, expressing it, letting it go. I worked on the Healthy Me watercolour while sitting with my corset brace and using the hospital utility cabinet table. Though quite naïve – I like it. Does my body get the message that I am watching out for it? "Body, are you listening?" (See Plate 6.)

I used the same coppery colour of the chemotherapy for the butterfly wings – wings of transformation, and filled them with wonderful symbols of joy, balance, protection, rainbows for optimism, love and laughter.

Then I meditate, paying attention to my breathing, my body, imagining the party, the farewells to cancer cells, and me, joyously looking very beautiful, filled with "hostess with the mostest" vitality.

Day four

I worked on this watercolour and began a new one – expressing my feelings about the chemo. It has calm, soft, beautiful, flowing colours. I totally surrendered to the process, visualizing the violet flame of trans-mutation[1] and the copper-coloured fluid working together to create wellbeing. Mandala forms appear, creating symmetries, unification and balance. (See Plate 7.)

I feel myself slowing down. It is a strange process to experience moment by moment. The time passes well. I have a great sense of love surrounding me – a presence. It must be my party. I doze off.

In the wee hours, I took out Eckhart Tolle's book A New Earth, which I began months ago. I opened it randomly to a place where he talks of being aware of one's body from the inside – a sense of inner space and presence. I felt as if Tolle wrote for me, to help me know what I "know". I thought, "Yes, I've been there, sensed that, the 'presence', the 'inner space'." These simple words let me see it clearly.

Day five

I begin the last bag of chemo, which will finish tomorrow morning. I am looking at the end. It was a very calm, pleasant day with a few joyous highlights: a real shower, breakfast sitting in a chair, assisted excursions to the bathroom.

I observe the flow of me . . . my sense of quiet, peace and joy. When I sense discomfort, I place my attention on that area of my body and "see" it absorb all the wellbeing and healing energy that I know is just waiting to be called forth. I imagine it there. I imagine it felt. I imagine it calming and I am calm.

As I let go I feel a passion stirring. I must not let this feeling dissolve. With all my seclusion, I have a sense of touching my world so precisely. I feel so much love. It has been a strangely wonderful day.

Day six

The chemo ended! Hurray!! Tamir, the oncology nurse, took out my vein connection and now I have TWO tube-free legs! How nice to be walking around leashless! I have really not experienced many side effects from the chemo. I feel full and powerful . . . Ready for the doctor's rounds and then, hopefully, a shower and release.

Day seven – the body never lies, 4.41 a.m.

Yesterday, I went to get my discharge papers, all dressed and packed and ready, and was talking to Tamir at the nurses' station when I suddenly felt dizzy. He asked if I wanted to sit down as he scooted a chair behind me. Just in time as I collapsed – lost consciousness – fainted . . . I couldn't believe it. When they said that they wouldn't release me all my calm disappeared. I actually said, "NO WAY!" I think I threw a little temper tantrum, which is so unlike me (or not?). I wanted so much to go home.

Immediately they gave me intravenous liquids –as if I could lack fluids –and took blood tests. I was weak and dizzy for hours. My body had informed me of what I was capable of and forced me to completely surrender to another reality . . . I felt so frustrated. I wanted to go home and get into MY shower.

I drew myself fainting. The dots above my arm are parts of my consciousness being dispersed beyond the bounds of my body. I felt broken and helpless. Soufa came for a visit, helping me find the "beauty" of being so weak that I had to surrender. (See Figure 9 below.)

It's almost 5 a.m. I feel clear. I am writing from a distance. I was so out of focus. Why does my body want this? Natural processes are taking over. My eyes are closing. The sky is still black.

11.20 a.m.

To prevent another fainting episode, I was told not to stand up or lower my legs before they wrap them with elastic bandages. I have already drawn, nibbled an apple, almonds

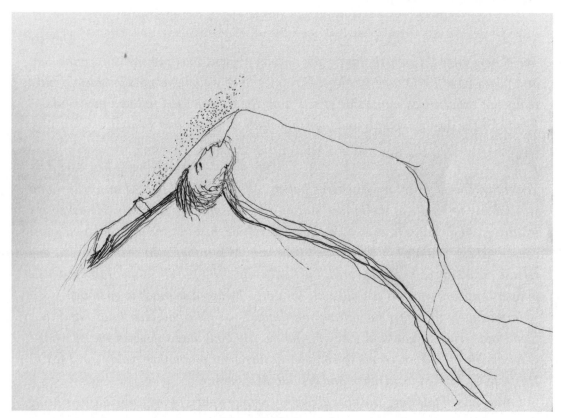

Figure 9: *Fainting*, ink

and some cake. I am losing my patience. No one has come to wrap my legs yet, so I am still stuck lying down. I haven't even brushed my teeth properly. Now I just want to be able to sit in a chair and walk to the bathroom. I am losing my patience.

I was journaling just because there was nothing to do and my emotions were beginning to boil. When I started complaining on paper I realized it was the victim in me that was getting angrier, fuller with self-pity and more frustrated by the minute. I saw the pattern of the powerless victim role I was caught in and wondered how to change direction.

Instead of encouraging my anger to boil and my victim pose to remain intact, I decided to act and called Tamir, and nicely asked him to wrap my legs, now. He smiled and he did. It was simple, actually. Now I will sit for a while, drink black coffee and go to the bathroom. What a small thing to put a smile on my face. I am mobile. Life is sweet.

Later I leave the hospital and return home. Tomorrow is my birthday.

PRACTICES

Practical doing and a che-mother-apy meditation

My seven days of moments wove a tapestry of joy, pain, love, anger, appreciation, disappointment, agitation, calm, creativity and passion – in short, life. Here are some insights that may be of help. Choose what fits you.

- **Breathing mindfully** really does ease difficult moments, helps coping with pain, fear and uncertainty while minimizing suffering (see Chapter 20, page 144). Remember the Murakami marathon mantra: "Pain is inevitable. Suffering is a choice."

- **Journaling and drawing** facilitates "being in the moment", in the "zone". They open a stress-free place to just be and flow in a lovely calm. At present I work in several hospitals in a project paid for by Roche Pharmaceuticals – Roche Lends a Hand – guiding meditations and offering mandalas to colour before and while people receive che-mother-apy. These activities recharge batteries, reduce stress and energize patients, caregivers and accompaniers alike. And it feels wonderful too.

- **Filling moments with joy** can be quite a challenge but it is possible, even when hospitalized or when receiving chemo. Creative activity, reading, TV, visitors, etc. can be considered distractions or can become the focus of a conscious desire to fill moments with as much joy as possible. It is an attitude choice.

2: *Burning Pain* (client drawing),
watercolour

3: *Stressful Time* (client drawing),
watercolour

4: *Coping 1* (caregiver drawing),
coloured pencils

1: *Some of the Pain*,
watercolour

5: *Coping 2* (caregiver drawing),
coloured pencils

6: *My Recovery*, watercolour

7: *Chemotherapy*, watercolour

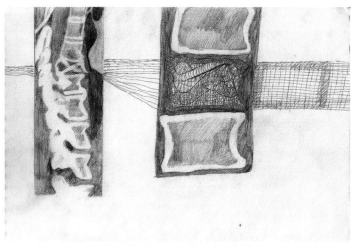

9: *Irradiation*, pencil and gold ink

8: *Manipulations*,
coloured pencils, pencils and ink

10: *Back-building*,
journal sketch

11: *Spine Work*, coloured pens

12: *Transforming the Spine*,
ink and watercolour

13: *Soul Song*, mandala
painting poem

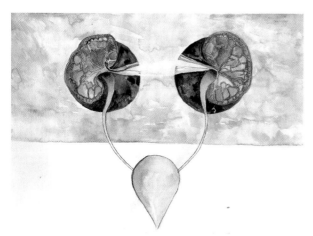

14: *Kidneys and Bladder*, watercolour

15: *Letting It Out – Feeling Pierced in the Back*,
ink and coloured pens

16: *Kidney Slice – What is Floating Away*, watercolour

17: *Kidney Slices – Deep Cleansings*,
watercolour and ink

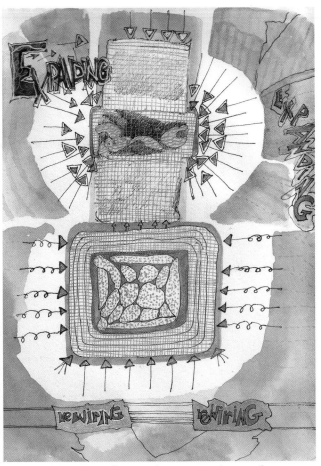

18: *Rewiring and Expanding,* watercolour and pens

19: *Mandala Drawing,* watercolour and ink

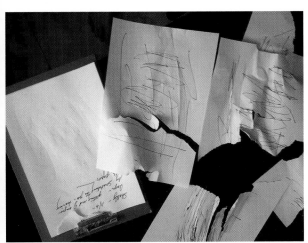

20: *Client Expressing Her Anger,* pencil

21: *Client Painting the Anger,* watercolour

22: *Facing the Distress Within*,
watercolour and black ink

23: *Retaining Fluids*, pencil

24: *Floating Up*, pens

25: Yael, my Jedi angel

26: Losing it

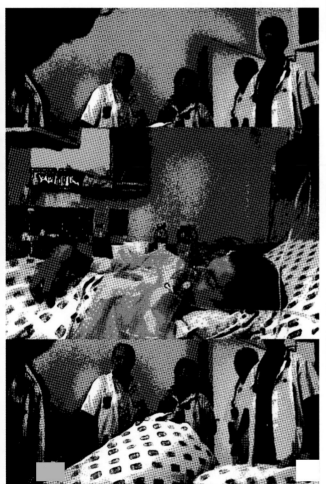

27: Being watched over

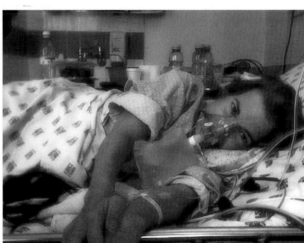

28: Eyes wide open

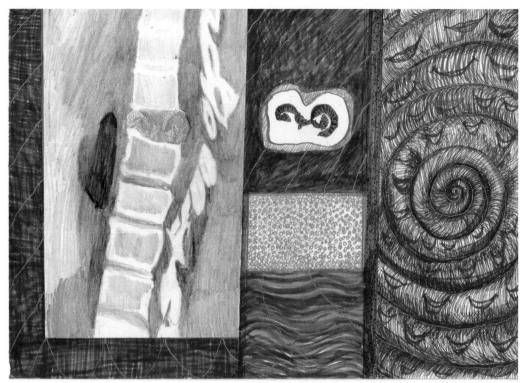

29: *Smile Energy into the T8*, transformational drawing, mixed media

30: *Finding the Light, Looking Through the Darkness*, watercolour

GUIDED MEDITATION 3 - CHE-MOTHER-APY

Before you begin this meditation, it's good to remember that chemotherapy – or che-mother-apy – can be thought of as "mother energy therapy" and biological treatments can be thought of as "life therapies" (bio = life). Words reflect attitudes making the treatment a bit more palatable. It is good to do this guided meditation before, during and/or after your treatment. Consciously focusing on releasing and replacing cancer cells, this meditation is fun and always ends in a big smile.

You'll find the text for this guided meditation in Chapter 21 (page 157) or listen to an audio recording at www.judyerel.com.

NOTE

1. A symbolic image used to visualize change – to transmute – or transform from one state of being to another like in the alchemistical transmutation of straw to gold. As they "burned" in the violet flame I focused on the transmutation of my cancer cells to healthy cells and the problematic patterns in my life to those that promoted my greatest health and wellbeing.

Chapter 8
April Realities

Wednesday, 18 April 2007

I feel weak, weaker all the time. It is my birthday, a big birthday but definitely not a dream birthday. Some close friends arrive with the most obscenely expensive, rich and delicious gourmet birthday cake surrounded by heavenly cookies. These were rich moments in total abundance, but very soon I became so weak I needed to be helped upstairs for the night.

A BEACHED WHALE

I awakened the next morning hardly able to move my arms, let alone my body. I was totally helpless, a beached whale. My caregiver, Carolina, had to feed me and I was back using a bedpan. I was so weak I couldn't move; I had no strength to even sit up. I barely ate. I called a healer friend who worked with a conventional medical doctor schooled in Eastern medicine traditions. They came to see me and gave me Tibetan herbs to build up my chi to rebalance my body. I was in the present, in complete surrender; there was nowhere else to be.

The next day was better.

By Saturday the beached whale was out to sea again. Yes! I was in awe of the way the body heals as all efforts – conventional, spiritual and alternative – worked together.

Time passes.

April flows towards May. Time passes. New routines are born. Time passes. I walked, tried to grow stronger, visited doctors, and did what I must. Independence Day came and I celebrated with friends at a big barbeque with lots of food, wine and laughter – a day off for almost normalcy. I was asked how I feel and I remembered the book *The Four Agreements* by Don Miguel Ruiz. The first agreement is to "be impeccable with your words"[1] – for words create. So I answered impeccably –"Better and better every day". I knew this was my truth . . . in the long run. I repeated it all day long.

Time passes.

The side effects of high doses of steroids were nerve wracking. I drew several circles on a page and tried to graphically describe what I felt. The first circle, showing the circular boundaries that couldn't hold its contents, reflected uncontrollable emotional outbursts that just happen. The second circle dealt with boundaries differently. Here the circular form was totally ignored, reminiscent of the feeling of having no boundaries when I fainted. The third showed several circles joined together as if they were ready to burst, reflecting my feeling like a balloon filled with water. (See Figure 10 below.)

After I vented my frustrations by defining these different sensations, I relaxed as if my plate had been cleared. I was ready to move on to face my back.

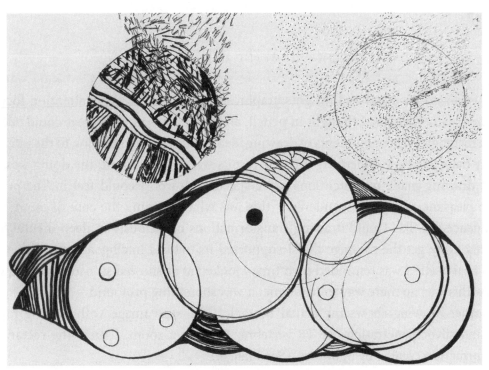

Figure 10: *Effects of the Dexa*, ink

DRAWING INTENTIONS

I reread my journal entry with ideas for healing my back using my CAT scan images as a reference point, drawing my back repaired using gold and tissue paper. Obediently, I printed out different views of my spine injury that were on my computer and looked closely at what happened. Now I understood what was referred to as a nasty collapsed fracture. The square vertebra was squished in various ways depending on the view.

I drew a schematic spine with rectangular vertebrae and copied different angles of my collapsed T8 vertebra from several CAT scan photos. They are the abnormal shapes on the pink background. Then I drew ways to turn the vertebra into a normal rectangular shape. I drew the stages of "repair" with enjoyment and ease. Not expecting anything except just to have some quality time with my vertebrae, I played with coloured pencils, pencils and ink. (See Plate 8.)

ANCHORING REALITY INTO INTENTIONS

As I visualized my ideas and insights graphically on paper, I felt my attention focus in my body, with my body. I thought in pencil, and drew ways injured areas could become whole rectangles. These moments of drawing ideas anchored my attention to the intention for my back to heal wonderfully. Artistic results weren't important; the doing was. The act of drawing made my intentions more specific, clearer. I could feel it. The process felt so pleasant, so right, I wondered if this was what touching the core of mind–body intelligence felt like. Could drawing transformations consciously in deep mental focus help my body get the message that I supported its natural intelligence and believed it could heal itself? I was reminded each time I looked at or showed someone the drawing. I knew this was no mere way to pass time; it was something profound.

Another drawing shows my actual thoracic CAT scan image with healing rays of gold and silver penetrating the T8 vertebra. As if in a zoom, I drew the rectangular transformation created by light rays. (See Plate 9.)

As I drew, I felt at one with the building process, with my back re-creating itself as healthy. After much consideration I reached my own precise definition of what I considered a healthy back – full functionality and zero pain. I didn't care if the physical bones changed their form – I just wanted them to act and feel like they did.

Time passes. I feel strong. Time passes. I feel weak. Time passes.

PRACTICES

Gaining insights and creating intentions

The practices for this section focus on releasing expectations, tuning into your intuition and bringing your intentions to the forefront of your mind to assist your healing journey.

- **Release expectations:** Once you start chemo, or other medicinal treatments, the body reacts. You don't know what to expect from anything anymore – especially yourself. This is a time to release expectations of what you can, should or usually do. It's time to stop comparing now with what you did before. I decided that I had no desire to suffer anymore and would be glad to let that go, and my narcotic pain regimen supported that reality. Treat yourself as if you were your own child and know that "this too shall pass". You may find some friends are there for you and some may surprisingly disappear. Again release expectations and try to be grateful for those who are there and know that those who disappear are dealing with their own fears and problems. It's not about you.

- **Listen to your inner voice:** Ask yourself, "What would you suggest to someone else?" And let your intuition guide you. You can write, try to

---

understand and, if you think you can face things better with someone else's help, find someone to support you in your decision to actively deal with this problem. Most hospitals have psychologists and social workers and some have additional integrative medical services, and there are always people like me who have been there, done that and are now working to help others face such challenges with a winning mindset.

- **Connecting reality to intentions:** Are you beginning to see a method in this madness? Reality can be connected to intentions through active doing that translates ideas into something physical, whether they be words on a piece of paper or a drawing or, as I mentioned earlier, any nonverbal creative expression or activity that stirs your imagination. You can even use routine activities like washing your hair or taking a shower as symbolically washing your illness away. Imagined, focused thoughts open new connections and possibilities when aligned with action. I found myself intuitively repeating and re-clarifying ideas, desires and images. The detailed repetitions plus the substantial time spent in pleasant, creative activity kept my energy very positive and intensified the momentum of focus. Now I invite you to list some of the things you like to do and think of how you can use each one to visualize healing your body.

NOTE

1.   Don Miguel Ruiz, *The Four Agreements*. San Rafael, CA: Amber-Allen Publishing, 1997, p. 25.

Chapter 9
May Flowers, Routines and Realizations – Looking At What Is

I barely noticed how my days have jelled into set routines – waking, pill taking, showering, creams, foot rubs, dressing, blow drying my hair, eating. Each movement requires attention, effort and Carolina's assistance. Nursing care is no longer new. It is what it is. It, too, is routine. As Carolina holds the hairdryer I dare not lift, I turn the brush in my hair and marvel at the grace in which formerly solo activities became routine cooperative efforts.

Almost nothing from my "normal" life remained. Though my days were full, there was no role to play, no identity to hide behind; I felt naked. The brace I wore said it all.

Changes of atmosphere and attitude

My daughter Yael and her husband, Avner, arrive for the summer. They fill the house with laughter, light and music.[1] I am thrilled that they will be in Israel until mid-August, at which time Yael begins teaching again at Pratt University. They surprised me with a moleskine journal to write or sketch in, the kind used by Hemingway and Picasso. I interpret this gift as a sign of unlimited possibilities. Writing to capture thoughts and sow seeds of intentions, the ink flows effortlessly onto the fine, smooth paper.

Words become a declaration . . . a prayer.

"I release all ties to anything but joy and love. And as I do so my back gets fuller and fuller – rebuilding itself with joy. Amen"

Doodling my vertebrae's reconstruction tickles my creative power. As I transform broken bones on paper, I signal – no, tell – my body that I want to heal and how I want to feel; I reinforce and strengthen it with gold ink. Old cells die; new cells are born. Continuity is created by intelligent cell memory. I want mine filled with joy because I truly believe joy heals. (See Plate 10.)

I ventured to consciously touch the place that Mom tapped into and Deepak Chopra[2] calls the core of mind–body intelligence. I constantly strived to align my mind and body with the conscious intention to heal remarkably well and repeatedly called-up an image of a normal statistical curve in my mind. I imagined a chart of all the healing possibilities and potentials – from no healing at one end to complete healing at the other. I visualized myself at the extreme positive end, instinctively knowing not to let anything I say or think cloud this vision. I figured if Mom decided that ONE chemo series would be enough then I can decide to heal my back and my blood with my treatment protocol.

Check-ups and insights

Yael drives and I am an impossible back-seat driver; which is ridiculously comical because I can't even see the road – the front seat is totally reclined leaving me a view only of the treetops, sign-tops and sky. I'm trying to control something, anything, but everything is out of my control. I feel very apologetic, but – like Dennis the Menace – it just happens.

While Yael and I waited for hours at the orthopaedic and haematology clinics, I realize something profound: I have 24 hours to fill each day and they are the same hours no matter where I am. What's more, I always fill them perfectly. My power is how I feel when I fill them.

Hours are just a measure: hours, minutes and moments. I've always known that but now I knew it differently. I could enjoy or be stressed out, I could be curious or bored wherever I was or whatever I was doing, it had the same meaning from time's point of view. It was the same – it was just being – it was just being me. Yael waited calmly; she came at this time to be here with me, for me. It didn't matter where. I realized I, too, was doing what I was supposed to do – to just "be". Now I was just "being" at the outpatient clinic. It didn't matter how long we had to wait. I could "be" wonderfully impatient, be perfectly apathetic or be joyous. I couldn't fail. I could always be me perfectly. My choice was how I perceived these moments of being. My decision was easy; I was finally with my daughter Yael and that was wonderful. I wanted my being moments to be a joy.

My orthopaedist told me the x-rays also showed a collapse in the T10 vertebra, the T8 was unchanged and that movement was important for my back. My haematologist said my blood responded very well to the chemotherapy. Things were progressing.

CHECKING WITH LOUISE

The T10 vertebra, according to Louise Hay, was connected to needing to blame someone and be a victim. The patterns of victimhood, shame, failure and lack had to be very deep if they affected my physical body so profoundly. I realized this was no one-shot deal – no single meditation or drawing could wish this away or make everything OK. No, this was a project to be reckoned with repeatedly and from as many angles as I could think of – physical, spiritual, emotional and creative.

So the next day, I went for a two-block walk to my neighbourhood supermarket with Carolina; I walked at a slow pace, visualizing my back getting stronger with every step. I never thought of walking from one end of the supermarket to the other as exercise, but it was now. Of course I didn't dare lift anything from the shelves, but I could choose, point and lift my credit card. Carolina did the rest gracefully. Independence is a relative thing and I felt filled with accomplishment.

I no longer have the luxury of not clearly defining what I need or letting fear influence me. I know I must find my way to feel totally backed by myself. I'm still not sure what that means, but I observe myself, feel and act upon my needs. I feel very weak so I shall begin requesting and receiving reiki healing treatments to support my efforts. I'm tired now. I am actually falling asleep, touched by a connection with my Self that keeps losing its name.

Playing around with some of the coloured pens that Yael bought at my request, I worked on my T8 again. When I finished I saw something weighing heavily on my spine, which, despite its bright colours, pushes it into collapse. Are these the tensions that influenced my back? There is a woman there, looking backwards, running up a ramp. Is she trying to escape something? When she reaches the top will the spine crumble? At the time I didn't think – I just drew. I drew and moved on. (See Plate 11.)

Looking for and finding insights became my most profound routine. It became a state of mind. I observed; I examined everything for joy, significance and keys to healing. It felt good to fill my days with meaning. Everything surrounded this new "health situation", sadly enough it was also routine to be sick.

PRACTICES

Creating life routines

What routines in your life, both new and old, give you joy? Think of ways to make the not very happy situations better. What gives you joy in general? It can be visiting a park or the beach or the grandkids; or doodling, listening to music, meditating. Try to increase the fun aspects, decrease the annoying aspects and look for some way of enjoying the stressful situations being ill places you in. I know it isn't easy. But it is possible. You can put meaning into anything.

GUIDED MEDITATION 4 - SEA OF LIGHT

This general energy boost is a great meditation to make into a routine as an everyday activity or to enjoy while you are waiting for doctors, treatments, etc.

You'll find the text for this guided meditation in Chapter 21 (page 160) or listen to an audio recording at www.judyerel.com.

NOTES

1. They brought me one of their whimsical lamp creations (see www.lightexture.com) that complements the music that filled the air, see www.king-dancer.com.
2. See Deepak Chopra, *Quantum Healing*.

Chapter 10
Che-mother-apy II

It was again time for another 96-hour che-mother-apy treatment. The many emails, phone calls and responses to my first virtual farewell party revealed an effective addition to my treatment protocol. Wanting the clarity of my intentions to renew their echo throughout my world, I re-affirmed my decisions and choices carefully in the present tense.

Subject: Update and invitation to virtual farewell party #2
To: Everyone on my mailing list
From: Judith Erel
Sent: Monday, 7 May 2007 8.53 a.m.

Hi,

I begin this update with some really good and encouraging news. Partying is good for my health! The results of the last chemotherapy session and virtual farewell party were excellent! There is a very significant decrease of pathology measured by my blood tests. My haematologist is very encouraged!

That's one good reason to celebrate and the other is that it's time for another chemotherapy session SOOOOOOOOO I am inviting you to my second Virtual Farewell Party Bidding farewell to the cancer cells in my bone marrow as they leave my body, aura, and energy forever!

I choose to see this as another wonderful opportunity for me to open myself to the care and support I know I deserve . . . I choose to see myself in total wellbeing, with joy, love, flowing creativity, perfect health and enough money to have whatever I wish. Cancer cells don't suit my life; they have no place in my world. For me, they contain all that is not love, joy, wellbeing or abundance. They are connected to disharmony, wild growth, victimhood, lack and suffering. These cells do not reflect my Self or my life. They are appreciated for any good that they may have brought my way, but are thanked doubly for knowing that they are moving out of my body and aura – never, ever to return.

You are invited to virtually celebrate, aid and support my farewells.

How? Just use your imagination – even for a moment any time from Tuesday, May 8th, late afternoon to Saturday night 12 May. Imagine, pray, send a thought, love, light. Imagine me happy, and with the help of the chemotherapy, bidding farewell to these cancer cells, thanking them for the part they played in my life and seeing them released from my body and aura forever.

A classy friend of mine ordered cases of fabulous virtual Claret wine, I have a great virtual caterer – there will be the virtual music of your choice, dancing and all in pleasant surroundings and happy colours. As usual, I'll be dressed in the very flattering, hot pink, polka-dot Assaf Harofe Hospital pyjamas clinking virtual crystal wine glasses. "L'chaim!"

Please invite any loving friends to my party, too.

I thank you for being part of my life.

Lots of love,

Judy

Day one

Yael came with me to the hospital and everything was easier. The IV port went in painlessly. I have the window side of the room and a manageable IV trolley so I can actually walk to the bathroom at will (with my brace, of course). What more could I ask?

Yael organized my books, paints, pencils, pens, paper and glasses so I could reach them in the cabinet while lying flat on my back and left me her iPod prepared with meditation music that I love. I am listening now, feeling at peace and at home with myself. She's been an angel.

All day we focused on situations: the tests, tasks, organization, now, alone, I turn my focus within – to the coppery, translucent che-mother-apy flowing through my body.

I think of my back; pick up a pen and a sketchbook and draw on the orange, yellow and red watercolour forms I painted yesterday. Using a printout from my CAT scan as a model, I sketch my spine precisely in the upper right section. I begin with my physical reality, the CAT scan. As I draw I feel as if I am entering my body and touching the bones. I see the collapsed vertebra from another angle – it looks nothing like a square.

How can I transform this? I wonder. What would I do if I could Photoshop it? Ideas fill my mind and I smile. I would use Photoshop commands of free transform and then skew it or stretch it pulling the top and bottom apart. So that's what I do.

On the left side of the page, I draw the transformation; first the top contour line, copying the shape from the CAT scan – then I leave an exaggerated space underneath and draw the bottom contour line. I s–t–r–e–t–c–h the side contours of the T8 image to meet the new top and bottom and fill the inside with gold stretch marks. Black arrows border the rest of the orange rectangular shape indicating the direction of pull. I do this intentionally, s–t–r–e–t–c–h–i–n–g the collapsed T8, feeling the lines become part of my intent, my consent, my body-mind, my will. (See Plate 12.)

In another orange square I use arrows of golden ink to p u s h the shape out further and finally create it again as a normal-shaped rectangle filled with gold and silver spaces, cells, energies. In the lower right I fill the damaged T8 and T10 with silver light rays to cement it into a normal shape.

I imagine energy particles of light and consciousness from my intentions uniting with my back. As I draw, I feel, I know that my pen and its magic transform the physical world at a non-physical level.

I don't waste my time or energy wondering if it will work or if I am being weird. I just draw and do what the voices I "heard" during radiation told me to do. The moments of drawing are fascinating, calming, and even joyous as each new idea becomes known. I don't expect or need to prove the power of my thoughts to anyone. I don't need to see changes in the x-rays, I just want my back to function normally and without pain. I plant the seeds of health and water them at every opportunity. I think of my art as transformative rather than descriptive.

Now I am ready to greet my guests at the Virtual Party. All the guests: family, friends, colleagues, teachers, students, loves, all those in my pasts, present and futures – as well as all parts of my Self including the instigators of uncontrolled cells that mistakenly protect me from something.

I think about the anti-immune quality of my illness. I evidently create rogue antigens[1] to fight some unknown, erroneous threat that ends up hurting my own body. I wondered how this super defensiveness in my cells was reflected by behaviour patterns in my life.

What am I trying to protect myself from? Do I know my true boundaries? Do I fear being taken beyond them? Does this reflect a fear of revealing my true self and being rejected? Do I see my mistakes and failures as what I am? Am I asking myself the correct questions?

A definitive correct answer wasn't important; understanding, feeling, sensing the simple, yet complex unity of the body–mind and mind–body was. A new perspective touched my awareness, one that saw cell behaviour reflecting mental, emotional and psychological behaviour.

I write, I find myself teaching myself – one step at a time – as I step into moments of touching the "being there", in that special "here and now" zone of presence. I relax into the sounds of Paul Winter's album Canyon Lullaby. *I look at the coppery liquid flowing into me and smile, knowing I am being purified. There is a dance of beauty and joy releasing the fear and uncontrolled creations of dis-ease and disharmony with a gentle certainty that these cells and their consciousness leave my body forever. I shall create myself anew, with certainty and cleanse myself with a copper hue creating what I call a "new energy balance".*

Day 2

Time passes.
  By 9.18 p.m. the second bag of chemotherapy has ended. I sat in the chair with my legs up most of the day with a severe water retention reaction. My normally bony feet are puffed-up like a giant, fat infant's feet . . . I laugh. My whole body is so bloated there are no wrinkles, even when I smile. Otherwise I feel great. I'm full of energy and a sense of power. My day is filled with the right proportion of visitors and drawing.

I drew a word mandala with a poem spiralling outward, focusing on my intentions, clarifying them, making them physically visible. They seemed to flow onto the paper. I embellished the words with faces, hearts, smiles, spirals of energy and flowers. The captivating coppery colour encircles a rainbow. (See Plate 13.)

Oh Self,
The centre of my being flows with the light of love and unity.
There is a song being sung:
a song of courage and joy;
a song of choice . . .
a song touching my sacred heart and mind
where all is pure awareness, pure now,
pure consciousness, knowing Life is beautiful.
Life is joy. Life is creativity;
Life is abundance. Life is total wellbeing.
Life is love.
All that is not love finds no place in my songs.
For I am life.
I sing the song of my life each day anew
And today I choose Love, again.

It's party time. I "see" myself clink wine glasses with friends and bid my cancer cells farewell! I declare my intentions as if for the first time. "I am made of all that supports love, all that is plenty and abundant, all that is joyous and flowing, all that promotes wellbeing, loving, giving and receiving. All situations and people drawn to me support this path." I visualize myself beginning a wonderful new chapter of creativity that is reflected in my world. All that doesn't fulfil this intention and vision knows it must leave my cells, energy and aura now. I "see" it lifted. I "visualize" the cell memories that create these unnecessary cancer cells gently lifted from my DNA. I "imagine" them floating away in the flood of fluids engulfing my cells in the perfect rhythm for my highest good. Goodbye negative energies, bye-bye destructive memories, shalom cells that don't contribute positively to my life. You are transformed and transmuted to places and dimensions that can no longer touch my life with pain, lack, self-denial, self-destruction, powerlessness and fear. Farewell forever! I am thankful we are parting ways. I imagine situations that caused this physical result as things separating from my being and my physical, mental emotional, spiritual and energetic bodies forever.

I clink glasses – I imagine a big party crowd sharing my pleasure and supporting my journey to total wellbeing. I feel so very close to me. I am all and part of all. My magnet is my smile at myself. I open myself to the love and support my world offers. My over-defensiveness and fears fade, disharmony leaves my body, energy and aura. I visualize the un-love, un-happy, un-joyful, un-healthy parts separating, taking bows, being applauded for their decision to leave me. I imagine them enter the violet flame of transmutation and become neutralized cosmic dust ready for recycling.

Waves of love, gratitude and bliss flow into my heart and in the background I feel the cheering support of my virtual guests. I "hear" the virtual music and the clinking of crystal wine glasses chiming l'chaim. I feel so honoured and grateful feeling this passion and just flowing with it, "L'chaim – to life."

Day 3

Friday is a slow day. Avital came for a lovely visit. I am retaining water throughout my body, I feel humongous and uncomfortable. I laugh at myself with no wrinkles anywhere! My legs feel like they may burst. I've been given diuretics, first in a pill and now intravenously – but the situation has its own timetable and improves very slowly.

What is this need to hold on to so much water? I know that the element of water represents emotions, and is now trapped in my body – filling every pore, every cell. Maybe I can see it as a pressure rinse from the inside – washing away all the aspects and memories that I have asked to be cleaned away? The process is uncomfortable, difficult, even painful. It's time to go to bed as it's hard for me to sit in the chair.

Day 4

In the wee hours of the morning, I awaken from a short sleep and chat with Smadar, the night nurse on her rounds. I complain about the water retention . . . I can't help myself.

"Why are you so angry with your kidneys?" she asks, rather than verbally easing my discomfort or being sympathetic to my misery. "You shouldn't be angry with them – you should give them the time you need."

I am blown away – Smadar asked one hell of a question! She didn't say "they" need, she said "you" need. I feel my understanding shift. I try to sleep with this question in mind. Perhaps I dare not look at all the deep memories and patterns I am trying to dissolve, so I am trying to float them away en masse. Must I wash every nook and cranny within me? Evidently my process needs more space and time, especially since my intention is to create a healing solution that will be for my highest and greatest good. Again I muster up all the trust I can in what is: I see myself calm my impatience, make peace inside, forgive my totality, my perfectionism. Can memories, feelings, emotions be washed away?

The iPod plays music with the sounds of gentle waves. In my mind's eye I create a celebration of farewells to the memories, intentions and the old choices being washed away. Gratitude wells up inside me for all the angels that cross my path with gifts that touch my world, and reveal hidden mysteries of myself. Solutions and directions for inquiry peek out to lead me to another truth.

I just began the last 24-hour bag of beautiful chemotherapy. I am dozing off . . . thankful for all the support I feel. It's time for the violet flame of transmutation to do its work.

Day 5

It's now 1 a.m. and I finished the last bag of chemo about half an hour ago. Time does pass and today went fairly quickly. I am weaker from the diuretics, the release of retained water and I guess the treatment itself.

Accepting the rhythm rinsing my insides and emotions, I feel the victim inside, the suffering tied to being a perfectionist, for judging the best I can be by external standards. I realize that this declaration, intention and promise I made to myself over 20 years ago – to be the best that I could be, should be tied to my own definitions of best only, and even that can change moment by moment. Will I be able to make that leap?

I know my efforts have a positive outcome, whatever the results will be. They will be positive because that's the way I have decided to see them. I focus on the now.

I begin to feel motivated, energetic – the upside of the dexamethasone. I start to think about a new series of drawings – my kidneys.

REALIZATIONS

Writing the pre-chemo email updates and invitations reinforced my commitment to myself, kept me in touch with my support system, filled me with renewed motivation and gave me somewhere to go during the long hospital nights. Partying is so good for my health. ☺

The mind–body dialogue focused clearly on my vertebrae, my bone marrow, emotions and uncomfortable situations, like the need to reduce water retention. Activities like journaling and drawing helped increase my awareness of what was going on and suggested additional factors yet to be understood.

An attitude of looking and finding was so important. Life doesn't just fade out into another scene when you get the point. With all the steroids in my system I slept only two or three hours out of 24. There were a lot of moments to be filled and many were in discomfort. I did my utmost to see everything as happening for the best, although I purposely defined what the best was very loosely. As I observed myself, I noticed that if I looked at things with the right attitude, I could find something useful, interesting and transformational almost anywhere. For example, imagining retained water as washing away whatever needed to be cleaned from my cell memories.

Words and ideas that came up seemed to repeat themselves again and again: in a poem, a prayer, a thought, a note to myself, an email and/or a drawing. Evidently "getting the point" wasn't the point. There were repetitions because at the time "they" were real again, relevant again, and part of a now moment again. Being in a serious reality of imbalance and trying to balance a body with cancer needs more than one magical drawing or visualization to transform it. I believe repetition helps reach the depth needed to create the transformations I aimed for. I went by rule of thumb – if it came to mind, I did it again, if not, not.

I practised my routine of acceptance and loving what was.

PRACTICES

Focusing on positive solutions

Some doable things to try:

- **Focus on positive solutions** for as long and intensely as you can. Expressing this solution physically, verbally or nonverbally clarifies your intentions, emotions and thoughts and it also takes time. According to the Law of Attraction the more time you are focused on a particular thought or idea, the more momentum is created with which to pull that idea into your reality, for good or for bad. Drawing, writing, sculpting or imagining tied to some physical activity increases the time focused on the "solution" or creative result. Creatively expressing health draws health into your reality. If you sculpt mashed potatoes you can even eat your way to health. ☺

- **Expressing the solution** is a way to tell your body what you want. This process is described above in several drawings where I drew the CT scan of my spine and its healing process. You can use copy paper, tracing paper or paste part of your CT scan printout. There is no problem not "knowing" how to draw. Then transform what is unhealthy into a healthy body part.

- **If you have a growth,** you may want to draw the shape in pencil, then erase it again and again and again and then fill the problematic area with gold and/or smileys. Or use watercolours and then add water until you dissolve it, wash it away. Imagine it disappearing, getting thinner, less and less. You can even draw it on a piece of paper and burn it. Another possibility is drawing the blood vessels that support the growth and then draw ways to close off their line of nourishment line or cut off the blood supply. You can even cut the paper at that spot with a scissor. Let your drawings show how your natural healing intelligence is working with your treatment. Use these images to "see" it happening in your mind's eye and your physical eye over and over.

GUIDED MEDITATION 5 - CHE-MOTHER-APY FAREWELL PARTY

Enjoy a celebration filled with gratitude and love to mark this phase of treatment. You'll find the text for this guided meditation in Chapter 21 (page 161) or listen to an audio recording at www.judyerel.com.

NOTE

1.   Antigen: a substance that stimulates the production of antibodies.

Chapter 11
Reality, Reflections and Mood Swings

My tiny world swings in all directions. I came home from the hospital feeling a bit hungover, but strong. Yael and Avner, newlyweds who were originally planning to spend their summer honeymooning in India, have moved to a rented apartment close by. Avital is with me as much as she can be, despite her two jobs and a family with two small children. My house is my mirror. Avner installed all my handicapped accessories and repaired everything he noticed without my even asking. So as I was being fixed, so was my house. I was touched and very grateful.

Then I found out that my attached-row-house neighbours were deliberating a massive renovation to remove the old, dated, stucco exterior finish and re-insulate and refinish the exteriors with state-of-the-art materials and a modern look. I felt threatened at the thought of being forced into expensive renovations, especially now when I wasn't working. Though I knew the changes were sorely needed and would raise property values, I didn't want to face another complicated situation. Yet I also knew that if I didn't renovate with everyone else, my house would stand out shabbily and the property value would definitely be affected. Thus, another mirror and focus for cleansing, renewal, uncertainty and expense tilts my emotional balance from threatened to frightened to panicked, as personal buttons are pushed.

Over the next few weeks my steroid medications aggravated or perhaps created exhausting mood-swings between joy, gratitude, appreciation and insecurity, fear and anger. The content changed but the background of medicated "instability" reigned.

Alongside the little dramas in my life, I was trying to be real with myself – with no discounts. After all, I was filled with water, the element of emotions and was being challenged to accept new places in myself – some positive, some not. Soufa remarked that perhaps I needed to cleanse the areas between the cells, but what was between the cells if not more cells? Does that take me into the body's inner space? And what is that?

THOUGHT WORK TAPESTRY OF JOURNALING AND DRAWINGS

Feeling a bit lost and needing to focus my attention, I turned to my routine of expressing and anchoring my thoughts in action: Thought Work. Grappling with the water/emotion retention raised my curiosity – I wondered what was I dealing with? I found Internet images of a kidney section and the bladder, and drew respectfully, lovingly remembering my wee-hour conversation with Smadar, my night nurse angel. (See Plate 14.)

The gentleness of this drawing is reflected in my journaled thoughts . . .

Monday, 14 May 2007 – night – calm

It was easy to be in me today. I was conscious of being gentle with myself. I didn't even know what that meant a few months ago. I thought that being gentle meant being gentle to others. I learned that being gentle also means being gentle to me.

Then some hours later, my emotional rollercoaster took a sharp turn.

Tuesday, 15 May 2007, morning – major mood swing

I'm losing it. I'm losing my boundaries and control. I am facing walls. I rage and anger inside. I look to myself, past relationships and reoccurring behaviour patterns . . . I fume at myself . . . my inability to see clearly, being too gullible and my inability to see my boundaries and say "no". Too many times I let myself be manipulated or was afraid to say "no", because I was really afraid to anger, disappoint and be rejected. It was safer to open myself to hurt.

This has been a hard day of crying and letting things out, releasing and trying to be whole and real at the same time. I draw. What does being pierced, stabbed in the back, look like? Feel like? Each line is filled with hurt, anger, rage – a clenched jaw and grinding teeth. (See Plate 15.)

Wednesday, 16 May 2007

The day was full – but the emotional intensity and mood swings that seem so pathological take me by surprise. I blew up at one of my neighbours, who I like very much, about the neighbourhood renovations. I wanted to release the emotions and whatever needed to be washed out of my kidneys. I pasted a black-and-white internet image of the inside of a kidney into my sketchbook and then painted the kidney fluids. I call these paintings Kidney Slices. *(See Plate 16.)*

There is something poetic about trying to ease water retention with watercolour. I painted emotions with dark colours, like muddy waters. I sensed I didn't have to be aware of the why, what and drama behind emotions. There was no need to think in words. The colours spoke and I could feel "things" being touched. I wondered if they were muddy enough. Was the painting still too pretty? Was I not facing something?

When I began the next painting I was in a different place, as reflected by the lighter and less-biting colours. Without prior planning, this painting showed different "slices" or aspects that seemed to spiral off – and hopefully out of me. (See Plate 17.)

Afterwards I felt much calmer . . . cleaner.

Accepting what is and that it's all tied together.

The neighbourhood committee decided that the exterior of our 12 connected houses will be totally renovated. Another level of renewal was to begin. Everything is so synchronized and obvious even though I tried to deny it. The head of the neighbourhood committee will be contracting the whole project, which will make everything cheaper and easier (for me). All I have to do is pay and that touches a sore spot at this time when I am not working. My mother will give me a loan. I hate being needy. I guess if I was able to be so strong and fearless regarding my illness, something else came up – financial insecurity – to encourage me to release the fears and vulnerability hiding inside me.

I had another healing session with Haim (energy healer, reiki master and good friend), who told me that something around my chest needs to be released. I feel such heaviness there.

In the midst of difficulties there are also little celebrations – being with the kids, grandkids, friends, eating out, watching the sea. I smile with joy as much as I can.

I feel like I am drying up. My hair looks dead. The roots remained the same colour since March – nothing grows . . . it just gets thinner and thinner.

Thursday, 24 May 2007

My body echoes sensations, feelings grow more defined. I acknowledge what is as I write . . . And as I feel, I breathe . . . into . . . my back and . . . create . . . a new kind of support . . . grounded in gold . . . silver . . . and copper strands of light. Later, I drew and painted the expansion and rewiring of my back. (See Plate 18.)

Whenever I breathe mindfully I enter a quiet that turns into visualizations. Anything in my life can become raw material to work with. Sometimes it's a thought, sometimes a journal entry, sometimes a drawing and sometimes a combination. It didn't matter how it started or whether it began from something good or bad, it seemed that these days I could always turn my thoughts into a now that healed, cleaned, calmed what hurt and supported healing potentials. As I put my thoughts to work – Thought Work worked proactively. Doing Thought Work focused on my back helps me get past this seesaw of moods and feelings.

Saturday, 26 May 2007

I feel cleansed. I painted a mandala that filled me with new feelings – feelings of gathering disparate parts together, adding complexity and more empty spaces creating a new balance and unity. I am surprised and enjoy the lyrical beauty. (See Plate 19.)

Sunday, 27 May 2007

Again I feel bloated and overwhelmed by my reactions and emotions. My washing machine broke down. All this water retention and now even a washing machine filled with clothes and dirty water is my mirror.

PRACTICES

Creating routines and overcoming overwhelming mood swings

Taking responsibility for emotions. I invite you to think about your emotions:

- Who takes responsibility for their existence?

- Does what the "other guy" does or did to you cause the emotions? Are emotions just waiting for a button to be pushed – of love or anger?

If you wish to take responsibility for your emotions, that implies the emotions are yours. They come from you, even if medications let them out of their cage or situations create dramas that help you see them, release them and/or fight them. They are in you.

Sometimes finding the emotions you want to express can be an experience in itself. Here are two drawings from clients I have worked with. The pencil drawing is that of a very sweet, soft-natured woman with multiple myeloma, who couldn't admit to herself that she had any hard feelings or anger at all. Using a pencil on computer paper, she touched her feelings. Her anger was very deeply buried. She was so moved after she was finally able to release her feelings that she began to giggle and filled with pride. (See Plate 20.)

The next example is from an ultra-religious man who joined my activity in a hospital where I work. He asked me if I could help him release anger. He told me he was so filled with anger at everyone, himself, everything, God included, and that he even forgot how it felt to smile. I was taken aback. I gave him some paper with a large circle on it and some watercolours and instructed him to put his anger in the circle on the paper. He painted slowly with small strokes and deep concentration. When he completed his drawing I photographed it to document the process. Then I directed him to rip his painting into tiny pieces and throw it into the garbage, in a kind of ceremony. When he finally left there was a smile on his face and tears in my eyes, along with many others at our worktable. I will never forget this. (See Plate 21.)

- Be kind and gentle to yourself. When you become conscious of emotions like anger, frustrations and intense mood swings you can take the mindset that these emotions have arisen from so that you can see them and then release them. Of course it's better to release them harmlessly on a piece of paper rather than snap them out on anyone else or yourself.

- I invite you to use visualizations, imagery and/or creative action to express your physical, emotional reality as a tool to help release what needs to go. You can use guided meditation to release the tensions and emotions and fill those areas with joy and tranquillity.

GUIDED MEDITATION 6 - A PERSONAL PRAYER

This meditation expresses what you feel and plants the seeds for a future you . . . how you want to feel . . . and the moments you create as the unification of the mind–body–spirit heals disharmony, separation and conflict.

You'll find the text for this guided meditation in Chapter 21 (page 163) or listen to an audio recording at www.judyerel.com.

Chapter 12
June Celebrations and Darkness

Subject: Update and virtual invitation #3
To: Everyone on my mailing list
From: Judith Erel
Sent: Saturday, 2 June 2007, 8.51 p.m.

Hi,

Time is passing and I am in an intense process of healing from within. Since the last chemotherapy I have been energetic with relatively few side effects. Following my orthopaedic doctor's instructions I walk around my neighbourhood each day and feel stronger and stronger. The brace I wear gives me some freedom of movement, which I feel is growing. I am on a narcotic pain regimen so there is little to no pain. What can I say – HEAVEN. I have been doing visualizations and drawings – re-creating, rewiring, expanding and rebuilding my T8 vertebra. I am doing the best I can to enable the possibility of getting through this without undergoing surgery . . . and luckily I have a conventional orthopaedist, who believes that it can be done. From his purely medical view he expects to see results in a CAT scan in a few weeks. I am certainly working energetically and spiritually in all the ways I know to make it happen!

On the cancer front – tomorrow, Sunday 3 June, I will check in to Assaf Harofe Hospital for another 96-hour slow-drip chemo. It will be the same, beautiful copper-coloured stuff that I had the last two times. And again I invite you to join me for a virtual bash.

Please join my virtual farewell party to bid farewell to all the energies, cells, memories and even dependence on elements that have caused/ created/ influenced this cancer. All that has not given my SELF the honour it deserves. During the past month I have learned new ways to love myself and my world. Join me now in loving and honouring the SELF and releasing all that is not connected to joy, love, honour, abundance and respect for the beautiful being that is me, and you too for that matter. This thread of beauty and purity is a most joyous reason for celebration.

For over 100 hours, the finest virtual red wine will fill our glasses, marvellous gourmet dishes will titillate the taste buds, amazing music, atmosphere, dancing, stand-up sessions, clowns and acrobats will virtually enhance universes and of course, very special pink polka-dot pyjamas will add a smile of fashion.

Love you and thank you for being in my life.

You may invite loving friends too.

Love,

Judy

Writing invitations to this third celebration was revitalizing. I purposefully focused on my strength as I recapped the positive from May to June. Although there were many complexities, I tried to put them behind me as part of my healing path. I truly believe that everything happens for the best.

Sunday, 3 June 2007

It's the wee hours of the morning and, after a usual first day of hospitalization, I am amazed how used to these routines I have become. Now all is quiet, I am alone with time to focus inward. I feel myself being.

I ask for and take all virtual energies supporting my efforts with me on the path to rebuild my T8 and my T10 vertebrae. As I write I visualize the disintegration of plasma cells involved in the uncontrolled growth in my bone marrow. I have a deeper understanding of who I am. I envision myself becoming less systematically afraid of invasion and threats, which perhaps mirrors the autoimmune reaction of an "overprotecting"/vulnerable immune system. I envision manipulative situations not working, and imagine them disappearing. I will them away as I close my eyes, envision my party, and the dancing, laughing, wine glasses clinking, joyful colours, smiles filling my vertebra, my bone marrow and my cells.

I drew to get to the bottom of my feelings and an abstract colourful ink drawing appeared. It was my usual positive side presenting a smiling, optimistic face – but I felt it to be a mask. I realized there was something more. The emotional swings have uncovered something that I sensed was hidden underneath the "happy face me". Could I dare let it come through on to the paper? Intuitively my hand reached for a fine black ink pen and begin covering sections of colour, creating something new – it felt more real. I look at what peeps out, trying to get deeper . . . closer. I was feeling strong enough to allow deep points of emotion to emerge. And emerge they did.

Wednesday, 6 June 2007

Three days have gone by or should I say thousands of moments, time passing. I am very weak, low key, following myself, observing myself. I'm told my washing machine totally died. I, too, am filled with fluid and heavy, unclear emotions. I meditate trying to heal the heaviness in my chest. It's the same place that Haim worked on two weeks ago but now it physically hurts. Could this be connected to the darkness I've been drawing? I've been working on the same drawing since I arrived, adding layer after layer of black, trying to touch something illusive. I wish the chemotherapy would wash it away. As that desire becomes conscious, I begin visualizing: "seeing" a shower of light going through me, rinsing away the hurts, the shadows. I feel so quiet inside . . . more than quiet. I feel FLAT . . . Empty. "Let the distress dissolve, disappear, be washed away."

The drawing was completed after four days. Each day I felt the need to cover the original colourful drawing with more layers of fine black ink lines. Did I find what I was searching for? Was I drawing more denial? Was I hiding things after planting them or letting another truth be seen? (See Plate 22.)

The heaviness on my chest won't go away. Is that what I am drawing? I wondered what else I could do. Knowing that forgiveness heals I tried the Ho-oponopono "I'm sorry – I love you technique" to work the heaviness out of my chest. I had to forgive myself for creating situations that caused my pain. I could feel myself releasing blame and anger. I could feel the heaviness dissipate for a while but it returned. It was deep and pervasive.

Friday, 8 June 2007

It was a long night. I finished the chemotherapy around 1 a.m. but I was up almost all night with tremendous pressure, pain and distress on my chest.

Before it was time to go home, I made a pencil drawing of me, bursting at the seams. (See Plate 23.)

Saturday, 9 June 2007

At home – a quiet, gentle day. Not much strength. I am so super sensitive – touching ground, painful ground, hurting ground. Then some friends come for a visit and my weakness fills with smiles.

Sunday, 10 June 2007

I am quiet in the house. Not moving much. I feel worlds of feelings and sensations tied to feelings of anger and frustration. I calm myself by drawing them. (See Figure 11 on the following page.)

I saw facing and accepting these feelings as a sign of progress and strength. I was facing my dragons head on.

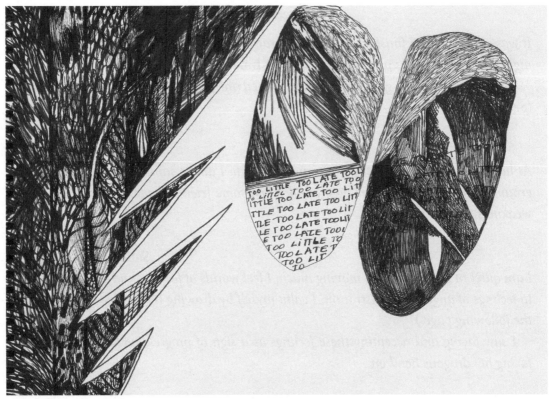

Figure 11: *Too Little Too Late*, ink

Chapter 13
Dragons of Doubt and Death

Monday, 11 June 2007

I feel very loose . . . can't hold on. Don't want to hold on. Can I let go a little? Let go of what? I don't know what is keeping me in this world. Doubt. (See Figure 12 below.)

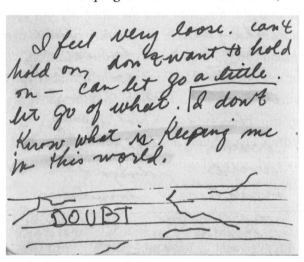

Figure 12: Cracks in My Wall of Strength, journal entry and sketch

Two days later I was hospitalized with a high fever and what was to become a mortal encounter.

Monday, 2 July 2007

Doubt crept in.

I questioned my desire to live. Why? For what? Oh, I know I love and am loved by my children and grandchildren, but I also know that that isn't my reason to be alive. How will I start my life over again sick and weakened? Create financial security? Get back into the normal world? Find new love? I was losing it – losing my vision of life.

Four days after chemo I developed a high fever and was told to go straight to the Assaf Harofe Hospital emergency room. I was hospitalized immediately; an infectious disease specialist was called in; all my doctors and more were in consultation. Yael was there daily from morning to night. Avital was there every moment she could. I was in critical condition and protective isolation; everyone was fighting hard for me. They checked for everything – viruses, bacteria, fungi, gave me many tests including a full body CT scan – and worked overtime to discover what was wrong. All that was missing was Dr House[1] himself. I was given a huge amount of anti medication – antibiotic, antiviral, antifungal and anti this, that and the other. My veins were weakened from the continual infusions of strong meds. In the end they ruled out everything they tested for and left me on broad-spectrum antibiotics. Meanwhile I continued to weaken. The fever wreaked havoc with my body. I couldn't breathe without a full oxygen mask. They were considering intensive care and a respirator and prepared my children as to the critical nature of my situation.

Was "this" the distress I was feeling and drew during the chemo? I wondered. Could that have been why I felt so weak afterwards? Finally a pervasive infection in both lungs and sepsis were identified as the culprits.

And I was sinking

When I closed my eyes I felt myself sink . . . slowly . . . stopping for a while . . . and then continuing downwards . . . slowly . . . I was underwater . . . in a lake . . . the Valley Stream State Park Lake, near my childhood home on Long Island (NY) . . . under the murky surface . . . sinking deeper and deeper. It seemed like this vision was in the background of my mind for a long time, maybe even days. I physically felt myself sink downwards, like on a slow-moving elevator . . . deeper and deeper into the turbid depths of a lake covered with blackened, rotting leaves. As the dead soggy leaves sank beside me, I noticed one orange-coloured autumn leaf afloat on the lake surface above. I watched the distance grow as I sank farther and farther away from it. I felt strangely calm.

Finally it came to me – this was it – I was sinking, separating. I realized that I, Judy, was in the process of dying. As these thoughts and visions flowed through my mind, I was not frightened – to the contrary, I was bizarrely fascinated. I heard myself think, "Is this what you want? Do you really want to die? Judy, you are going. Is this what you want?"

A calm discussion began. I felt a clear separation between Judy and "Me", and I sensed the profoundness of that moment. I felt quiet, even tranquil, and surprised that I felt no panic.

To be honest I was very nervous about living. I had no idea what life with a collapsed vertebra and cancer of the bone marrow really meant. How would Judy support herself, would the quality of her daily life ever be normal again? Would she ever be able to live independently with a decent life? Did I have the energy and real desire to cope with all that? I honoured the questions, knowing whatever the choice it was worthy and justifiable. I lay there just being, letting my heart find its truth.

I saw Yael sitting in the chair in the corner of the room. She had been sitting there all day, every day. I looked at her and I felt her love for Judy. I was aware that "I" would never die but Judy would. She was a one-time deal. In the reflection of Yael's love I realized what I was facing and how precious Judy was. I felt "It". I felt the love "I" had for "Judy". I didn't realize how much I loved her and believed in her. At that moment I knew for sure that I wasn't ready to give "Judy" up yet. There was more to do, to create as Judy. Then, I knew I must hurry up and turn this "thing" around before it was too late.

A decision, a clear choice of life came over me. I felt my Self physically turn the steering wheel 180 degrees. It took several turns of the wheel to feel a change.

The path going up was golden. My intention for life was clear, as was the change in direction I felt. I was no longer sinking . . . I was floating . . . upwards. I checked again and again to make sure. Yes, like an elevator ascending; I was still underwater, but floating up towards the surface. I see it in my mind's eye. (See Plate 24.)

Then I began to recover. The infection began to recede. Everyone, doctors included, let out a sigh of relief. The danger had passed, but the suffering and helplessness increased. Gadi arrived from LA a day after the turn around. Yael, Avital and Gadi visited and tried their best to make this difficult situation easier. I was calm – it was just a question of time – my decision to live was staunch.

More good news . . .

After seeing my full-body CT, my orthopaedist came with wonderful news: the bones had set by themselves and I could be without the corset brace! My lungs also needed me to breathe fully, so I was helped into a chair. I couldn't stand and could barely sit for more than a few minutes at a time because my core muscles were so weak from months of non-use. They burned painfully from the exercise of sitting in a chair.

I was too weak to eat, but I needed protein. So I ate nuts, a sardine wrapped with yellow cheese and drank something stronger than Ensure and very bad tasting. I fought for life through my stomach, but developed intestinal problems that cleansed me thoroughly. I remained in the moment of everything. The good thing is that moments pass.

I knew I was coming back to life and cleaning out what had to be cleansed. I had no strength to do anything creative but Yael and I did play with her computer, making fun photographs. (See Plates 25–28.)

Finally, after 16 days I was on the way home. This had been the most difficult hospitalization yet, but the drive home was markedly different – I was sitting up! When we came to our highway exit, I had an "aha" moment: I was so much in the here and now that upon seeing our exit I felt the "hospitalization" disappear into a distant past. What was no longer now, was no longer.

It was time to rebuild.

INSIGHTS OF A DRAGON SLAYER

While I faced my deepest realities – mortality, doubt, beliefs, fears and desires – in the midst of incredible weakness, I found self-love and strength. I also found a place honouring the choice to live as well as not to live. Being tempted by both choices I gained a new respect for life and for death.

I accepted my visions and sensations as aspects of reality . . . my reality. Maybe they were hallucinations, daydreams or maybe just my imagination – it didn't matter really. Whatever they were, they came from me – so they were real for me. They reflected my inner reality and lit the way for me to talk to me. I listened. I answered. I decided.

I knew the monumental choice I had been given required complete honesty and impeccability – it was a place of truth . . . There was more that Judy could be and do and I loved her/me enough to try for it. I made a commitment.

My back was healing as I intended!

I was doing my best, being all that I could be.

NOTE

1.   From the TV show *House*.

Chapter 14
Recuperation, Integration and Freedom

June became July.

I am sitting in my living room chair. Confusion, listlessness and disbelief still echo silently, "You almost let go." Something inside me aches. That place that must be found, loved, healed! I am fogging up – forgetting where I am – tears blur.

I want to be totally ready to create a new, healthy reality when I have the transplant to remake my bone marrow . . . Is there much more that needs to be released to make that possible?

I draw to release some of the feelings that haunt me, like the feeling of not having space to breathe . . . a memory from when I was in the hospital. I felt this struggling for air in my mind's eye then, but didn't have the strength to attempt to express it until now. (See Figure 13 opposite.)

I crave to do something constructive. So I draw my back, my smiles, and it feels good to be back at "work", focusing my thoughts, my power – strengthening my back, building the vertebra with gold and silver energy and earthy sienna brown smiles. (See Plate 29.)

I drew reds and oranges purposely to fill me with the warm sparks of life energy, but I knew I was not far from the darkness. (See Plate 30.)

I let myself go with the flow. Gadi, now living at home, was in and out all the time – sharing his optimism, laughter and joy easily. I know that all my children were dealing with their own emotions as they parented their parent, but we never spoke about it. I knew and I think they knew that I had to focus all my efforts on balancing myself. I was so glad that Carolina was the one taking care of my personal needs so they didn't have to deal with that also. I just focused on the immense joy I felt having all my children and grandchildren in the same hemisphere, and in the same room, laughing, playing and enjoying together. Just being with them and watching them together and

Figure 13: *Breathing Space*, ink

the love they have for each other filled me with delight. Delight is precious, not-to-be-wasted stuff, so I envisioned it going straight to my cells. Joy heals. Waves of gratitude engulfed me.

Mornings found balance, filling my soul with colour and feeling the joy and gratitude of being alive. The doing filled me with peace, pleasure and calm. I worked slowly; each drawing took four to five days to complete. (See Plate 31.) It was an enjoyable way to recuperate, find me sitting in my garden absorbed in drawing mandalas.

I notice that the copper colour has become an important part of my pallet and I loved it. It has become my personal colour symbol for healing and transformation. (See Plate 32.)

I play with the designs. Each mandala unites different elements and has a different symmetry and balance. Were these drawings reflecting my intention to be filled with health, balance, appreciation and harmony? I was deep in concentration without words. It was a nice place to be. (See Plate 33.)

I noticed the shift in colour choices and imagined my cells bathed inside and out in the strong colours with each touch of the brush. I figured whatever colour I chose was exactly what I needed. I wondered what that meant, but it didn't really matter. I worked slowly, enjoying every moment. (See Plate 34.)

I paint, I heal, I am in line and colour. (See Plate 35.)

Friday, 20 July 2007

Silence – even to myself. My body has been getting stronger but my spirit is still not steady. The feeling of mortality and knowing I was so tempted to let go is still present. Now I must muster up the strength and power to face the hardest process yet . . . the stem cell harvesting and bone marrow transplant. In six days I am scheduled for a full day of outpatient chemo – Yael will be with me, which should make things fun.

It's time to gather myself together to re-create an infallible attitude, but I don't feel the focus. Tears shed themselves at will. It has been hard for me even to write. I just reread my first entry. I wrote something then that should be in my mind daily so I rewrite it now . . .

"I am joy, love and health. I release all ties to anything but joy, love and health. I give and receive joy and love with ease."

A RETURN TO FOCUS

Update and invitation time again challenged me to be impeccable with my words. Being truthful, while keeping my goals in mind became a tool to reconnect and replenished my waning feelings of empowerment.

Subject: Update and invitation
To: Everyone on my mailing list
From: Judith Erel
Sent: Wednesday, 25July 2007, 12.32 a.m.

Hi,

I hope all is well with you and yours. A lot has been going on since I last wrote . . . so . . . here are some updates: I just saw my orthopaedic doctor today for my monthly check-up and my back is doing great! The broken vertebra has stabilized and is fixed in place – like squashed pitta bread – but fixed. The parts of the bone that extend near my spinal cord caused no neurological damage so I am really a success story that way and it looks like there will be no need to operate on my back, thank G*d. The doctor told me that I need to wear my brace only while riding in the car. I asked him what my limitations were and basically he said to go easy and gradually work up to doing everything I could. The key is to let my body's reaction be my guide. I can even start to drive small distances he said so I will try to drive two blocks to the supermarket tomorrow. Hurray! Freedom and independence is in sight!!!!

On the cancer front – the last chemo went very well as far as farewells go. Thanks to all those celebrating the farewell of my cancer cells with me. My blood tests show a large decrease in the myeloma and that is great and just what should be.

I know that it's been a long time since I last wrote and that's for several reasons. The good reason is that my son, Gadi, arrived and joined his sister Yael who has been here since May, so all three of my kids are close to home. A great reason to celebrate. I have had a lot of good family time and great gourmet meals that the kids love to cook.

The other reason is that, unfortunately, after the last chemo I was so vulnerable and my immune system so low that I developed a high fever and a very, very, very serious case of double pneumonia. I was hospitalized for over two weeks, and I must admit that I was thrown for a loop physically and emotionally. I am pretty much back in shape – just in time to start the last, most challenging journey.

On Thursday, 26 July, I will be going to Tel Hashomer Hospital to begin the autologus bone marrow transplant process (autologus means that I am my own donor). The first stage is to harvest my own stem cells, which will later be transplanted back into my body to build new bone marrow. I begin the process Thursday, as an outpatient for about 10 hours, and will receive a different chemotherapy treatment than before. I'm not sure really who's against who with this chemo – but I think the idea is to kill off blood cells in order to stimulate new growth. Then I will get several days of injections of a substance that stimulates new cell growth – especially stem cells – and throws them into the bloodstream. And then – and here's the whole point – I will go to Tel Hashomer to harvest stem cells in my blood. You sit in the Stem Cell Harvest Room in a really comfortable TV chair connected to what looks like a dialysis-type machine that harvests stem cells. The richness of the harvest determines how many times I will have to do this.

The next step – anywhere from one to two months after 26 July – I will begin the transplant process, where I will receive a mega-mammoth dose of chemotherapy that will completely kill my bone marrow and immune system. Then my own clean and frozen stem cells will be reintroduced into my blood to build new and healthy bone marrow. This entails hospitalization from three weeks to a month, partly with preventive isolation precautions and then a recovery period at home. The good thing is that at the end of this process the myeloma should go into a nice long remission. But that is still up the road a bit.

As for now, you are invited to celebrate with me at a virtual party beginning this Thursday from 7.30 a.m. Let's celebrate "the leaving of the old to make room for the new". It can be thought of as a pre New Year's exercise, like cleaning out a closet making room for new clothes. Renewal and creation of new cells should begin when I take the injections five days later. So all those who want to visualize me as letting go easily of all the old cells that served me well, and not so well – in faith that new, healthy cells can take their place with ease and in large numbers – are invited to do so. And while we are having fun with that please visualize me making loads and loads of stem cells that are easily harvested.

As usual – at my virtual parties the music, refreshments and wine will be the finest.

All are welcome – so come celebrate making room for new beginnings starting Thursday, 26 July and lasting about 10 days.

Cheers to all and may the force be with us.☺

Love and thanks,

Judy

Tuesday, 29 July 2007

When I wrote this last email update and invitation I felt my power surge back to life. It was amazing. It's like "Ta-Da . . . I'm back" but with a little more respect for my body, my Self – and less demands for perfection or achievement. I found compassion for myself.

These days Avital, Gadi and Yael are my teachers. They mirror my strengths and shortcomings. I love and am inspired by them. This is not a time of deep deliberation or introspection. I live each day as it comes, aware through my body, my art – through each line, each brush stroke.

I dance the days, enjoying the kids, grandkids Michal and Yonatan, enjoying painting and enjoying just being as I pass through the harder parts of weakness and self-doubt. The word "doubt" still isn't easy for me to write.

I began the transplant process last Thursday when I received the pre-stem-cell-harvest chemo. Tomorrow I begin the series of injections. Then on Monday I will go to Tel Hashomer Hospital to check the blood count and if possible begin the harvest.

Meanwhile, my hair is so thin. If it were winter I'd wear a wig, but the July/August heat is much too oppressive, so I arrange the hairs on my head the best I can.

PRACTICES

Finding joy, gentleness, diets and mandalas

The practices for this section focus on gentleness and allowing your creative impulses to flow.

- **Moments of joy promote health** so I invite you to focus on joys as much as you can, and that may mean going on a diet of nothing more serious and tense than Walt Disney and Barbara Streisand. (I mean it in a good way.) Be with those you love, make time for friends, creative activity, a good movie, a walk, the sea, feeling close to yourself.

- **Be gentle with yourself.** Anyone can lose their grasp on life, sense of focus and control, just like slipping off a strict diet or falling off a ski board and breaking a leg. Like dieting, one binge doesn't mean the diet is over, unless you want it to be. There is only a need to refocus. Composing an update and invitation in two languages did that for me. I consciously regained a grasp on myself and my intentions with every word I wrote communicating to others. What helps you regain your inner power?

- **Keep drawing and/or colouring mandalas**. The mandala format with its simple geometric beauty makes no demands to draw "identifiable" realistic images or think in words. You can use a compass and ruler to create a geometric mandala design in pencil. You can use coloured pencils, chalk or watercolours, or create a collage; you can outline chosen areas in pen and let your creative instincts loose. Let your colours and sub-patterns be chosen intuitively. If you wish, you can let designs within shapes appear to create complex places of balance. Studies have shown that adult colouring activity, whether in colouring books or mandalas, lowers stress and empowers the immune system.[1] Jung felt the mandala format touched one's innermost self very deeply and considered it the archetype for the self and individuation – the "path to the self". Each mandala you create is different and expresses your here and now.

NOTE

1. With over 1,000,000 hits on Google for "therapeutic effects of colouring", this is the topic of innumerable blogs, newspaper articles: i.e. the *Guardian*, the *Huffington Post*, *USA Today* and seen on Fox News and CNN.

Chapter 15
August: Collecting Joy and Harvesting Stem Cells

Since deciding that joy creates health, I knew this was the time to collect joyous moments to save for next month. I lightened things up with smiles and paint with watercolour intending to joyously release excess fluids. (See Plate 36.)

The purple paint leaked onto the next page of my sketchbook so I decided to discover what laughs can come from small paint stains . . . like the purple hats that surprised me in a light-hearted whimsical seascape /creature-scape that began from several small blemishes. (See Plate 37.)

Thursday, 2 August 2007
Speaking of hats, Yael and I went shopping for hats and scarves for my soon to be bald head. Without a brace I look normal, inconspicuous.

I do some automatic writing (a sort of brainstorming with myself by writing questions to myself and letting the pen just flow with intuitive answers). In this excerpt something very interesting appeared:

Q: Is there anything I need to know?
A: That you know. You know the paradigm of the Self united . . . to heal. Your words spread and touch and will be of influence. The raising of compassion levels allows the new energy to enter more peacefully and be absorbed. Passion and compassion must spread to enable a leap into the fifth dimension of reality.
Q: What is that?
A: Within the fifth dimension you create maximum wellbeing.

I reread what I wrote and wondered: is that the new paradigm – healing through uniting the self or when the self is united? What does that actually mean? And what is the fifth dimension? If 4D is 3D space plus time, does 5D have to do with intention? Causation? Manifestation? Does compassion, a quality of the heart energy centre, enable maximum wellbeing by helping energy to be absorbed? Must the heart be open to a certain degree to let positive energy in? The words seem wise, but I wonder what it all means down here on earth? The message to myself said to "know that I know", so I decided to keep doing what I've been doing with greater confidence and I picked up a pen to draw a mandala of joy and smiles. (See Plate 38.)

Harvesting is a wonderful word. What kind of harvest did I want? A happy one, of course. So I drew my stem cells, multiplying, smiling, happy, expecting them to get the message. (See Plate 39.)

Sunday, 12 August 2007

Facing the super cleansing and renewal of the bone marrow transplant procedure is scary but I have no mortal fear of this life-threatening procedure, because if it were my time, I would have gone last month. However, I am very nervous about the physical moments of the procedure. Moreover, I wonder if I will be able to follow through and keep the changes stable afterwards. I hope I won't forget, won't sell myself short and be a pleaser again. That's my biggest fear. My eyes well up with tears, telling me I've hit upon something. Can I really let myself be happy? Can I create a world for myself based on joy, love and abundance? Did my time of forced royalty being a queen and centre of attention teach me that I am worth it? That I can accept being so deserving?

STEM CELL HARVEST

My cells were harvested in two sessions on two separate days. I had to squeeze a ball in my hand to pump my blood continuously – for hours and hours. My veins are worn out; I am worn out. But the harvest was good. They harvested enough for several transplants. Hmmm, will I need several transplants?

It's time for another update, to thank all those supporting my efforts.

To: Everyone on my mailing list
From: Judith Erel
Sent: Thursday, 16 August 2007, 5.52 p.m.
Subject: Update

Dear all,

Just a short update. I have had a wonderful harvest, rich with stem cells that are now frozen, waiting for their turn to create new bone marrow and a "new" healthy me. Thanks for all your support, good wishes, prayers, thoughts and celebrations. Now I am waiting. This is a time when I can easily be among people and seem to feel stronger than I've been in a long time.

The next step is the big one – the bone marrow transplant with my own stem cells. It's the last big mountain before I reach the oasis of good health, where I intend to live for a very long time.

This will take place any time between two weeks to a month when my turn will come and the process will begin. I will send out invitations to the last set of virtual celebrations when they tell me it's time. Till then thanks again and enjoy the rest of the summer.

Love,

Judy

Saturday, 18 August 2007

Yael left for New York two days ago. I feel her absence sharply.

Just before she left, I finally took the leap into baldness. My hair had really been shedding – leaving clumps in my hand, so I decided it was time. My friend Ofra came over with her son's hair clippers and shaved my head. She chatted away the whole time . . . so gentle, so positive, so loving and with no pity. It was wonderful. (Two years later she told me that she was in tears the whole time.)

And then I looked. It turns out that I have a beautiful skull and pretty good ears. What a strange way to come to appreciate my face. The nakedness of a bald head is actually quite nice in the summer. I love the way it feels. Sometimes I walk around bald, other times with a large brimmed hat or a scarf. I feel like more masks are ripping away. Michal and Yonatan are in awe of my baldness and love to touch my smooth head. They pull off my scarf or hat to rub my crown and I let them. We laughed together when Yonatan got a really short, shaved-off-look haircut and I bragged that my hair was shorter than his.

I begin to visualize "my life after . . ." A new me to create a new reality – a different every day. I visualize sending energy to the future to open up possibilities for an exciting, new chapter. I even sold one of the mandala paintings I drew last month.

My days until D-Day filled. I focused on joy – collecting joy and happy moments. Then I woke up with a familiar, excruciating pain when I touched my side, it hurt to laugh and breathe deeply. It felt like my rib had cracked or broken during the night. Several days went by and the sharp pains remained the same. I knew there must be a reason – my body was trying to tell me something. It was so important to me to feel as good as possible before the transplant and I was so angry at this pain. I sat in my meditation chair and shouted to myself: "What the f**k do I need this for?" Then I closed my eyes and waited attentively.

I sensed a scenario, a setting, something like the Spanish Inquisition or Christian martyrdom. It wasn't an emotional scene, just a cool reference to not betraying one's beliefs. Suddenly I "heard" my own voice say very arrogantly, "You can break my bones but you can't break me." I laughed at my smugness. And then I knew, I understood.

I couldn't begin my bone marrow transplant without realizing that I am my bones: my bones, my body, my feelings, my thoughts, my beliefs and my soul are what I am – my Self – my beingness. Just as there are different parts to my physical body, there are different parts to the whole me: the physical me, emotional me, mental me, spiritual soul of me. All these mes can live in peace and unity or with hierarchical separation, indifference or war. It was imperative for me to see "me" as all my parts interlaced . . . equally important, together as one. This must be "the paradigm of the self united . . . to heal . . ." revealed by my automatic writings a few weeks before.

I realized that the kind of healing I was after could not be done on one level alone (e.g. body or mind). The Thought Work I had been doing was a way to unite the Self – seeing all parts of the Self as one creation working in unison for the Self's greatest good. With chronic cancer I would need to promote my continued good health and wellbeing on all levels, proactively. Was I testing the path to continued strength and recovery – long term?

So that was it. I had to begin the bone marrow transplant process with a deep inner sense and knowing of that unification. I laughed at my stupid ways of communication with myself through pain – but I guess I didn't hear otherwise. I let my anger go and wondered what else went on beyond my grasp.

Two days later I noticed that the pain was completely gone. Cool, huh? I love when that happens. ☺

As the bone marrow transplant approached, I was humbled by the depth and timing of what I was about to do. This was the most sacred time of the Jewish year, the High Holy Days – the Jewish New Year, Yom Kippur – the Day of Atonement, and I was physically facing a complete destruction of my immune system and the surrender of all my defences in trust of what could be. For me it became a time of impeccability, faith and trust.

This was the time to use tools of the spiritual guide, healer and author Dawn Clark.[1] Being familiar with her work I used her unique symbols for soul unification to unify everything I possibly could. I drew and coloured them in a mandala. (See Plate 40.)

She also has an interesting 21-day approach to manifesting conscious and unconscious desires by repeating positive affirmations. She claims that the effect on the unconscious increases if the affirmations are said while looking into a mirror reflection of your left eye. I wrote a list of what I wanted to create in my life and formed positive, present tense sentences. I repeated each affirmation three times in her three formats: "I deserve . . .", "I have . . ." and "I am happy that I have . . . " For three weeks I stated my list of desires, planting seeds of intention and watering them every day. For example: I am worthy of a healthy, pain-free body; I have a healthy, pain-free body; I am happy that I have a healthy, pain-free body. Some of my other affirmations added these phrases to each declaration: healthy, strong veins; healthy, cancer-free bone marrow; healthy cells filled with joy; a wonderful relationship with all that is in my body; healthy strong ribs; and a body that reflects the joy, health and vitality of my greatest potential.

Finally I was ready.

PRACTICES

Making choices

A few months ago, in a hospital where I work, I spoke to a sick woman whose blood pressure was in the sky. She was having a bone marrow transplant (autologus: using her own stem cells) the next day but because she was so anxious and fearful, she couldn't continue the procedures she came to do. The oncology nurse suggested I try to calm her. The woman was terrified by the life-threatening nature of this difficult procedure. My own experience of choosing life showed me the importance of bringing one's desire to live to a conscious decision. Facing this with clarity makes things so much easier. Among other things I guided her in a short meditation choosing life (see below).

- This can also be a time to look at what you want your new life to be, and not be: what attitudes, desires, habits and qualities you want to be reborn and what you want to send off with the "old you". I invite you to use whatever creative way you enjoy to express yourself. If you choose you can draw or write things you want to release and burn or bury them. Remember you are not trying to make something pretty; you want something authentic. It is the doing the counts. You can take pictures, make a collage or write lists of what you want to keep and be reborn to the hospital. Here are some drawings by someone I worked with before her bone marrow transplant. (See Plates 41 and 42.) The words she wrote in Hebrew mean acceptance, joy, spontaneity, love, beauty, childishness, sensitivity and ease. (See Plates 43 and 44.)

- **Collect moments of joy** to keep in reserve for the difficult time ahead. For me that meant focusing on enjoying every moment, having fun and being with people I loved, drawing with fun and bright colours, and taking time to relax and smell the flowers. Do things that you enjoy.

- **Notice how you talk to yourself and listen** – whether you use journaling, drawing, automatic writing or pain (my rib reminded me of what the Self united was).

- **Create "conscious intentions"** for the health situation you want by creating affirmations of your desired outcomes from the procedure. Repeat them daily. This is another way of connecting with the mind–body core. You can use the format mentioned above with three sentences for each intention: "I deserve . . .", "I have/I am . . ." and "I am happy that I have/I am . . ."

GUIDED MEDITATION 7 - CHOOSING LIFE

This meditation brings your choices to the forefront of consciousness making you aware of your possible choices. Your whole body will echo your choices as each cell becomes aware of your conscious chosen desires.

You'll find the text for this guided meditation in Chapter 21 (page 164) or listen to an audio recording at www.judyerel.com.

NOTE

1. See Dawn Clark, *Gifts for the Soul*. USA: Infinte Energylinks, Inc., 1999–2001.

Chapter 16
New Year, New Me

Subject: Update and invitation – the big one
From: Judy Erel
To: Everyone
Sent: Sunday, 2 September 2007, 5.45 p.m.

Hi,

Since my last update I have been concentrating on enjoying myself and I did such a good job that I filled boxes full of joy and happiness to use as backup for the next few weeks. Now I am just about ready to climb the last mountain to good health. Barring last-minute changes I will be hospitalized for a bone marrow transplant on Monday – tomorrow. On Tuesday and Wednesday I will be given mega doses of chemotherapy that will completely knock out my bone marrow and on Thursday – transplant day – I will be given a transfusion of my own, harvested stem cells which will then create new – healthy – happy bone marrow, new healthy blood cells and health. The process takes between three to four weeks with segments of protective isolation during the most difficult parts.

From another perspective I see this process as a wonderful celebration of renewal – the New Year and the New Me. Since bone marrow creates blood cells, whose flow is metaphorically the joy of life, I will be undergoing the ultimate renewal. For whatever reasons my bone marrow evidently had absorbed such disharmony that it created cancer – and became out of tune with the joy I am capable of. So now there will be a great cleansing enabling change and new healthy cell growth and joy. Perhaps my understanding is not medically exact, but the way I see it – not only will I come out of this healthy – but I will have an increased potential for joy as fresh new cells without past burdens nurture each cell in my body.

So what does all this have to do with the next party? Lots. You are invited to the biggest bash of the season – a virtual festival of the new, the fresh and the joyous – and just in time for Rosh Hashanah. Over the next three to four weeks (while I am hospitalized) you are invited to attend my Virtual Celebration Festival honouring the cleansing of my old and faulty bone marrow and welcoming the integration and assimilation of my new transplanted stem cells into my bone marrow. There will be virtual dancing, singing, stand-up, and of course virtual drinks and gourmet refreshments on the house – along with the best music you can imagine. The key words for this virtual festival are JOY and Celebration – for JOY is what heals. So please send me JOYous thoughts, wishes, prayers, healing and/or the energy of joy to surround me during this trek.

Join me in creating a New Year that Celebrates wonderful health and joy for us all. Thanks so much for being part of my life and my healing,

Judy

Throughout these months I had received many emails, phone calls, visits and responses to my updates and invitations. Just before I closed my computer the night before the transplant, I found myself extremely moved by words in an email from a total stranger (translated from Hebrew).

Shalom Judy,

I am Lilac's husband. I follow all your updates and your progress vigilantly and want to tell you how much I admire your fortitude and survival skills. With the coming of the New Year, I wish you health and joy with all my heart and pray you get through this time with ease. Your fighting spirit is enviable. Your emails reveal a strength that I am sure will get you through this wonderfully. There is nothing that is unattainable. I would be proud to follow you into any battle.

Be Strong,

Eli

I realized that so many people were truly cheering for me . . . even those I didn't know were there. I was taken aback and felt blessed as waves of gratitude filled my heart.

The next day Avital took me to Tel Hashomer. A port to a major artery in my chest was fixed for easy intravenous access. A turbo steam cleaner sterilized a room that someone had just vacated. Everyone in the bone marrow transplant ward had a sterilized, single room fully equipped with an extra bed for a caretaker or partner, TV, stereo, refrigerator and a private bathroom. It was about to begin. I tried not to be nervous. I brought art supplies, CDs of my favourite music, serious books and Harry Potter. This was to be home for a while.

Wednesday, 10 September 2008

I've been in the hospital since last Wednesday, 3 September. Everything is going according to plan – the intravenous port, the two days of mega dose chemotherapy, a half an hour each day that's supposed to kill the bone marrow, my immune system, as well as my hair cells, the skin in my mouth, the lining of my digestive system and who knows what else.

The next day, I was given a four-hour transfusion of my harvested stem cells. The medium maintaining the stem cells causes terrible nausea so after a few moments I vomited my guts out. Just then my friend Hava came by to visit and started to give me reiki. Amazingly I fell asleep. When I woke up, the transplant was over. There was no turning back. I was dying inside from the mega doses of che-mother-apy. My life now depended on the new stem cells floating in my veins to rebuild my bone marrow, blood and immune system. I knew my choice for life was clear.

And now I am beginning to feel the effects. I have no appetite, but I try to eat. My mouth is beginning to hurt. They give me a continuous morphine drip to counter the effects immediately and it works.

I am very calm and allow myself to ease into a safe space to imagine my cells peeling away and being renewed. I feel myself bathed in bubble-gum pink all new and happy.

I've spent hours drawing my intentions using Dawn Clark's affirmation format.

I look at a small mirror and draw it and the reflection of my left eye. I write my healing intentions surrounding the eye and mirror to create a word mandala that supports the health being created in my body. Like on my preparation lists, each thought was placed in the: I deserve (am worthy of), I have, and I am happy to have formats . . . so for example I wrote:

"I am worthy of a healthy pain free body, whose cells are filled with joy."

"I have a healthy pain free body, whose cells are filled with joy."

"I am happy that I have a healthy pain free body, whose cells are filled with joy." (See Plate 45.)

I drew this pencil mandala first. It took quite a while. The next day or so, I did it again in Indian ink. The result was harder, more defined. Everything's good. (See Figure 14, below.)

Then I drew a third, combining pencil, ink and watercolour . . . When I looked closely at the silver mirror, I could see how thin my eyebrows had become in just a few days. I worked slowly and deeply, painting the affirmations in warm, life-giving colours. (See Plate 46.)

Figure 14: *I Am Worthy of a Healthy Body Mandala 2*, ink

I feel myself in slow motion. I move, I think . . . I am as if in a different time zone. After this last painting I become too weak to create anything but myself.

I am thrilled that my back is really good – I don't feel like I have a back problem. I almost forget I am on a 24-hour morphine drip.☺

I feel a lot more relaxed being in the process than waiting for it to happen. I know things will become more extreme before they get better.

Rosh Hashanah – New Year's Eve, Wednesday 12 September 2007
The High Holidays are beginning. I am acutely aware of the significance this year. Avital comes by; others visit to wish me a Happy New Year. Gadi said he will go to holiday dinner late and we spend my holiday dinnertime together – though I can't really eat. We create our own spiritual celebration by articulating our dreams for the New Year and supporting each other's blessings and intentions. We have a deep talk of creating a year of choice. I am totally at peace. We ceremonially bless ourselves and each other and I am thrilled by the beautiful closeness we share.

As time passes things get more difficult and, before I realize it, someone is sleeping in my room every night, as Avital, Gadi and Carolina take turns. I am so weak. I am hitting bottom, I am in protective isolation so visitors and doctors have to wear masks and gloves to protect me.

I sit most of the day in a big cushioned reclining chair and am very passive. Sometimes, if no one is in the hall, Gadi takes me for a stroll along the corridor. I am so weak, he holds me up as we walk but I'm not in pain since the morphine treats me well.

My friend Dvora makes a cake with hundreds of eggs to nourish me even if I only eat crumbs. Ofra comes and feeds me like a baby with stories for each bite I swallow. I find myself fascinated and I actually manage to swallow some chicken and her silly stories. I think of myself as an infant, building myself from scratch. Avital comes every day. Gadi comes every day.

Gadi takes pictures, some I love. (See Plates 47–49.)

Some I don't. Gadi calls this next one the wise old sage. I see the "old". (See Plate 50.)

And some of such weakness and frailty, it hurts me to look at even today. (See Plate 51.)

Thursday, 20 September 2007

Ten days and a world away, and I am on my way out of "the process". My immune system is beginning to rebuild and everything is going in the right direction. However, the intravenous morphine that has made things easier, if foggier, until now was stopped. They didn't calculate that I had been on oxycontin for months, so when they stopped the morphine I began going through withdrawal – physical pain, hallucinations – the works. Thanks to Avital's being on top of everything, she brought it to their attention right away and I began a slow weaning period with low doses of oxycodone.

Home finally

I left the hospital on 25 September incredibly weak but whole. While I was hospitalized, the outside of my house was scraped and peeled and insulated, plastered, painted and changed. The neighbourhood looked like a war zone. Again the reflections were undeniable.

It was time for another changing of the guard. Now it was my sister Dale's turn. She arrived from Florida on 27 September to help me through the next very difficult two weeks and Gadi went back to his life in LA two days later.

Regaining strength and power is an all-encompassing desire. I could barely walk or eat but I had to – my weakness was boundless. Dale helped me build myself up. She cooked things I liked, took me where I had to go, was company as I slowly began to get stronger. I was so delicate – like a baby. It was wonderful to have my sister so close.

Finally it was time for another email but one I wrote with the greatest of joy.

Subject: Update and virtual invitation

To: Everyone on my mailing list

From: Judith Erel

Sent: Monday, 7 October 2007, 1. a.m.

Hi,

This is the email I have been waiting to write for over six months. Yesterday I went to my doctor at the Tel Hashomer Hospital for my second check up since the bone marrow transplant and I am officially in total RE-mission.(*Interesting word, huh*?) Medically, by definition of my blood test values – the disease is no longer active. The transplant worked wonderfully and this is the success that the past months have been aimed at attaining. I am so excited that I cannot sleep. (It's 1 a.m.)

I want to thank you for all the good thoughts, healing energy, light, love, prayers and virtual "L'chaims" that helped me along my way. Of course I realize that it is up to me to maintain the health of my wonderful, clean, light and healthy body for as long as possible to keep the remission going. I will do my best, believe me. And to start off right I wish to invite you to a virtual open house to celebrate the joyous occasion of good health with me starting right now. So "L'chaim" to life, health and joy. May we all drink our fill and dance with great abandon.

By the way – I am feeling better every day. I feel like a newborn – so I am taking it slow. My energy level is way below normal but growing each day and I am not restricted regarding where I go, visitors, or food. The only thing that I have to go by is how weak or strong I feel. I know that it will take time to get back to "normal" . . . but that's just a matter of time. Peanuts – no?

Have a great day and again, thanks for your support!

Love,

Judy

PRACTICES

Some ideas for the battle of a lifetime

During the procedure extreme doses of chemotherapy kill the diseased bone marrow and immune system. Aside from being difficult, you can see this procedure as a sacred, profound blessing. It is an honour to take an active part in giving birth to the new you by allowing yourself to become totally vulnerable, surrendering the old completely so you can become new, reborn with new stem cells to create a healthy you.

GUIDED MEDITATIONS

There are several meditations mentioned before, which are relevant at this time too, for example:

- Meditation 4 – Sea of Light (see page 160)

- Meditation 7 – Choosing Life (see page 164)

- Meditations 8 – Bone Marrow is specifically for the bone marrow transplant procedure (see page 166)

- Meditation 9 – Comradery meditation for those having donor stem cell or other donor transplants. This meditation is specifically designed to support the immune system, and can help make friends between the old and new immune systems (see page 167)

You'll find the text for all these guided meditations in Chapter 21 or listen to an audio recording at www.judyerel.com.

Chapter 17
Real Life Continues

Dale went back to Florida, the holidays ended and friends were back at work. Now that I was better calls were less frequent and visitors fewer. What filled and structured my life during my illness was changing again. I grew stronger knowing that my strength wouldn't be torn down by the next treatment, but now I was faced with rebuilding and recreating a new life . . . Again my external environment was an apt reflection. My immediate neighbourhood still looked like a war zone. My garden was in ruins, plants trampled, grass filled with cement and pebbles and the "finish" was taking forever. The house, garden, and patio were in upheaval mirroring my own renewal and slow healing process. I felt tossed in many emotional directions because of the destruction around and inside me

Time passes.

I face reality with little to soften the way – no more pain meds. My back is holding up but my muscles need rebuilding – I ache all the time. I'm not sure who I am anymore. Do the delays in rebuilding my external physical surroundings reflect the slow speed of my own inner regrowth? I sorely needed more patience.

CREATING A NEW WORLD FOR MYSELF WITHOUT ROSE-COLOURED GLASSES

Sitting in my family doctor's office, all happy with my remission status, another stark reality looked me in the face. My doctor said happily that now that I was in remission, "we would have two or three years of quiet."

"What?" I said, taken aback.

"Well, two or three years is the average time of remission before the myeloma acts up again," he said knowingly.

I reacted fiercely. "Don't ever say anything like that to me again. Do I look like a statistic? My health is not dependent on your statistical averages." He did not remain my doctor for very long, yet I realized that I would have accepted his reality as my own very easily if I weren't on guard. But what reality did I accept? What was my reality? After all, I do have what is called incurable, chronic cancer.

I have to face things as they really are. So I looked up multiple myeloma on the Internet – beyond Wikipedia. The prognosis was pretty good due to many new treatments available, but its nature really is to return – again and again. I didn't think about that until now.

Neither did I realize that bone marrow transplants don't automatically create remissions let alone total remissions. What I realized was that I still intended to be on the high end of the treatment healing curves and for me the sky was still the limit. It was clear that I had to find my key to keep this cancer fast asleep for a long, long time. I wonder what kind of lullabies my myeloma likes to hear.

I can't afford to be caught off guard again. It was important to be aware – all the time. If the myeloma wasn't busy snoring then it could be busy growing, so I accepted the fact that the remission was temporary. But I refused to worry about it because that would give my power away, so I decided to put a number on it. I thought 45 years or so is a good goal for a remission – 45 years, and then we'll talk (me and my myeloma) . . . I immediately signed up for my golden path for the duration.

I drew mandalas looking for balance and the sheer enjoyment of playing with colour. I worked very slowly, finding myself calmed in the process. Some of the mandalas I created around this time are shown in Plates 52–55.

I painted with fiery hues to get my fire back, knowing the hot colours were an expression of life energy. Then I drew an ink mandala to expand on it. (See Plate 52.)

The red and orange life energy blends with turquoise of healing and green of growth. First I worked freehand in colour and then I added the geometric divisions and then lines and patterns. (See Plates 53–54.)

I am like a newborn inside. Green . . . Spring, just beginning . . . Everything is so delicate, my skin, my hair. My scalp grows the fuzz of a baby chick.

When I am stronger I send back the hospital bed, another sign of positive growth. My living room is no longer a designated sickroom.

Mandala drawing is fascinating. It is a way to create balance and harmony – even in places of growing complexity. I see that as what I am doing in my body. (See Plate 55.)

By November my bald head was cold enough to make wearing a wig pleasant. It looked great and felt nice and warm. I was strong enough to try to work a bit so I went back to leading my meditation group at the Ra'anana Country Club, rejoined my old tai chi group, did physiotherapy and walked. By December my immune system was good enough for me to begin hydrotherapy in deliciously warm water. I received a treatment called Watsu – or water shiatsu – and just loved it! It became a golden path gift renewing a trust that my body was there to provide joy and pleasure and need not be measured by pain or the absence thereof. I found myself anticipating these weekly treatments and gained a sense of peace and joy in my relationship with my physical body for the first time since I became sick. I was now conscious of my body, my physical self, with a deep respect and gratitude previously unknown.

Sunday, 16 December 2007

Silence. This time silence means not wanting to even record the process – being distant from myself.

I feel so useless and like such a failure. I've reached another weak point. Dale spoke to me about the need for structure – and she's right. But I don't know what. I feel so naked – so wounded in my isolation. I am trying to get my life back into focus without rose-coloured glasses and I just want to cry all day . . . and I do. I find it hard to touch my centre to balance this storm. The days are short, but too long for me to fill.

As I get stronger, I need Carolina less and less. Soon it will be time for her to move on, which is pretty scary. Oh these challenges are never-ending.

Then Sari, a friend from my hiking group, who I hadn't seen in years, came by. It was wonderful to reconnect. Her significant other, a retired archaeologist, organizes weekend hikes and she enticed me to consider hiking with them when I'm up to it. Ummm.

Intuitive writing, or just talking to myself – no matter.

Tuesday, 1 January 2008

Slowly, slowly, let the shapes come forth to colour your days
Be there each moment,
Let the web form, send out its tendrils – catch its new balance.
As rebirth comes to being . . . you come to being . . . you are
being your dreams.
Make them good ones.

THE END OF A BEAUTIFUL RELATIONSHIP . . .

Every month I visited my orthopaedist for follow-ups. As usual he asked me to do various actions and I do them well. Another doctor entered the room while I was standing on one foot with the other knee raised in a very balanced "rooster" tai chi position. I continued to stand on one foot conversing easily with my doctor while the other doctor glanced at my x-ray on the computer screen . . . looked at me, then looked back at my doctor with a very confused look on his face.

"What was that all about?" I asked my doctor after his colleague left.

"Well, the x-rays and the patient don't match – when that happens our policy is to go with the patient." He answered, smiling.

Although the x-rays didn't reveal a new, perfectly shaped vertebra, my function level was exceptional and I was completely off painkillers.

"As far as healing goes, you're in the top 10 per cent," he said to me.

"Only top 10 per cent?" I questioned with a mischievous smile.

"OK, the top 1 per cent, I just didn't want to jinx it."

I smiled, feeling very happy with myself. But then he said that he didn't want to see me anymore . . . "Unless it was a happy occasion," he added, and that if ever I had any need he was there for me. I really liked this wonderful doctor and would miss him as another routine bit the dust.

Automatic writing questions and answers helped me to see the learning that treatment would bring.

Friday, 11 January 2008

Q. I'm looking for the voices - those that spoke to me when I was in radiation. Are you there?

A. Tune in we are here.

Q. What would you like me to know?

A. Trust, patience, getting stronger – that's what you are doing, learning. Preparing, all things you wish for yourself are possible – on their way.

Dear one, Dear one,

The ocean is opening and will reveal its treasures.

You are one of them.

Listen to the songs of your heart,

The truth of your reality at each moment,

Your purpose.

Walk the new path with joy . . .

Create this new path with joy.

Create with joy.

Ahh, life has its surprises

Inspiring by example.(Gadi's motto)

Tuesday, 15 January 2008

Carolina leaves. I want to panic, but instead I breathe deeply . . . and she is gone, taking my last vestiges of queenhood with her.

Monday, 21 January 2008

I'm really depressed, down, losing it. Avital (a clinical psychologist) convinced me to go for help, saying that with all the traumatic things my body has been through, it is not surprising that I have slid into a depression. I seem to be one inch away from tears all the time, I don't eat, don't sleep well, can't seem to fill my days. So I went to a psychiatrist.

I started taking anti-depressants yesterday. They will take at least three weeks to work.

I cry – what can I do but accept this place? I can't really find the joy.

A SURPRISE VISIT AND GUIDANCE

Do I deserve to suffer until the pills work? Absolutely not!

So the powers that be send me a wonderful gift to help shake me out of this hole. Gadi! He arrives on a day's notice for a modelling shoot he landed here in Israel. I love those kinds of surprises! He came in with a wind of joy, warming my heart and giving me strength. The house was hopping again! The first night he was here, he looked at me and said seriously:

"I have to tell you something, Mom. I didn't say it before because it wasn't the right time and I hope you take it properly now. Last summer you checked us out to see how much we loved you. You know that Avital is always there for you; Yael and I stopped our lives and came to be with you and for you. NOW YOU KNOW – DON'T DO IT AGAIN."

I laughed and thought – this kid is so uppity. But of course there may be a grain of truth so without another word I promised not to do it again and gave him a big hug.

Throughout the week we had many talks – including about my lack of focus and energy to create the life I decided to live for. He seemed to really understand my dilemma and showed me a technique that he uses with his career administration group at the Beverley Hills Playhouse Acting School in LA. It was exceptionally relevant guidance. Who knew I was to raise such an amazing man? I followed his method to organize and understand what was happening in my life and what I wanted to happen.

MY GADI PAGES

First he told me to make a Work Format Chart to organize my goals in all areas of my life: health, work, emotions, spirituality, attitudes, art and anything else. It looked like this.

Body – Health	Work	Emotions	Spirituality	Attitudes	Art
Walk or swim at least three times a week.	Write flyer to advertise art classes – send them by email	Be aware of feelings	Laugh every day (laughing yoga)	Read books	Mandalas
Tai chi twice weekly		Observe my reactions	Meditate about body and immune system	Do exercises	Oil paintings
Meditate	Edit Queen Esther painting series ppt	Give emotions less weight		Write pages and read them everyday	Poetry
Eat well			Visualize in the now		
Sleep well	Presentation to send out on the web				
	Begin to write book, copy diary entries, tell story				
	Think about exhibiting my art again and making it happen				

To put all the above ideas into a time frame, Gadi told me to create what he calls weekly creatorship pages. This is a way to connect desires to reality. In LA they work in a group that provides support and feedback. He knew that this wasn't something to do alone – so he said he would be there to give me the necessary feedback.

The following was my weekly list:

- **Gratitude:** List everything that I felt grateful for that week.

- **Did:** What I did this past week – writing, building my spirit, my body, my art.

- **I will:** What will I do this coming week – writing, building my spirit, my body, my art, etc.

- **Help I need:** In any area.

- **Help for others:** Any assistance I gave in any area to others.

- **Visualizations:** Dream big and let the stars be the limit.

It was just what I needed to refocus. Gadi told me to email my lists at the beginning of every week so he could comment and he did. His insights were incredible. If I didn't send it on time – he chastised me. Can you imagine? My baby boy, who never did his homework and majored in cutting classes, criticized me for not completing my assignments on time. I loved it. Life started an upward turn, my joy brightened and more joy came my way.

The lists acted like my update emails – writing intentions and committing to them revitalized and refocused me in the right direction. I realized the importance of "reporting" and committing publicly to myself – whether I was the public, one other person or an unknown number. The power was in the act itself.

I reconnected with an artist friend of mine and mandala teacher, Eitan Kedmy. He came to see my work and then sent others, including a woman who wrote an article about me for his website. At his suggestion, I took his mandala course to use his method for teaching mandalas myself. I began to reconnect to myself and life.

Then it became time to test my body. I took Sari up on her offer to go on a day hike to the desert – one of my favourite places. With mostly an archaeological orientation the excursion was not physically difficult, but there was a short wadi we would walk through. And I saw "the shadows". One of my favourite sights is the shadows of my hiking group falling on the ground or opposite hill. It is especially clear in the desert. When I saw "the shadows" tears welled up in my eyes as if an unconscious dream had come true. I thought I would never see them again . . . and here they were . . . the shadows . . . my normal life happening again. (See Plates 56 and 57.)

Monday, 7 April 2008
Time passes quickly. I am filled with joy . . . and my garden is finally growing. I am quiet, healthy, creating all the time.

I write intuitively, automatically, trying to touch that inner voice and this is one result:

"Sing a song of health to your cells
They love that lullaby.
Sing the song of colour to your heart . . .
It heals the scars.
Love is coming, knocking at the door.
Don't fear to open it.
NY, LA, FLA Rosh Ha Shana in the US

Celebrating a year since the transplant, I was off to the US for my first visit in two years to see family and dear friends. Before I left Israel, love did come knocking at my door and I "fell in love a bit", adding spice and roses to my cheeks in anticipation for the year ahead.

PRACTICES

Returning to life

Here are some understandings that helped me return to life. They may be meaningful for you too:

- Practise patience in the realization that there is no choice but to accept the rhythm of what is. You can't rush what needs time.

- Success means reaching the next challenge and being healthy means having to give up "being sick", which isn't always easy. The transition from sick to healthy may need a weaning period, just like getting beyond drug dependence.

- Some kind of organizing framework can be very important and create more intention, focus and commitment to life. If you feel the need you can use the life–work chart and creatorship pages that Gadi gave me. You can find them in Appendix III. It gives you things to do, lists to check off and a way to organize time. When you do more, the more is there to do.

- When you need help, it's OK to ask. One may feel that needing help is a sign of failure. Though we may want to be strong, the idea of accepting our own weakness can also be seen as a sign of strength.

- Smile, laugh, enjoy. Enjoy being in your body and be grateful for any little pleasure. It reduces stress and enhances the immune system. I didn't want to forget for a moment where I had been . . . it helped me enjoy where I was now.

Chapter 18
Two Out of the Blue

After that difficult year I got my life back: life, work, fun – lectures, movies. I went back to my hiking and study group and even hiked 10km up and down a mountain slope and across a wadi in the Negev desert where I saw lots of "those shadows". I loved how special and normal they were. I did tai chi regularly; I walked along the beach, danced and did other therapeutic exercises with gratitude to my body.

Work began to flow in my direction. By word of mouth, translations of meditation guides, art therapy and metaphysical work came my way. It was as if the powers that be not only kept me financially afloat, but pointed me in directions I should be aware of. Private students and groups showed up along with people who needed guidance. That's when I began to share what I had learned to help others cope with serious illness using guided imagery and my transformative art techniques. I gave inspirational talks about my fascinating experience, continued guiding my weekly mediation group, and sometimes taught art and mandalas individually and in groups. I began working in a programme supported by Roche Pharmaceuticals called Roche Lends a Hand, focusing on hospital patients waiting for doctors or treatments as well as during chemotherapy treatments, etc. I facilitated guided imagery meditations and brought patients mandalas to colour – which I still do today. I worked and played, enjoyed my kids, my grandkids (Yael and Avner gifted me with a third grandchild), my friends and even "fell in love" from time to time.

And then out of the blue – or more exactly, the blues – around 2012 things turned upside down. I had stopped taking my anti-depression meds, thinking I didn't need them anymore, and "crashed" into very serious depression. It seemed to take forever to rebalance. In addition I had been working extremely long hours on a big project with lots of pressure that left little time for my Self or any fun. During this emotional dark blue period my mother's health was also deteriorating until finally, in November 2013, she passed away. She was 91 years old.

Regular blood tests revealed that the myeloma was awake, though not yet at levels needing treatment. Then in January of 2014 a phone call from my family doctor created an extreme scenario I wasn't prepared for. He told me that my routine mammogram showed a small cancerous growth in my right breast. It was very small but I needed minor surgery to remove it. I wasn't really frightened for my life, but during the past year or so I had lost touch with my Self, my willpower and my joy, laughter and gusto. More tests were needed to locate the exact spot and rule out the existence of other malignant growths. Life took me into a super stressful time and on top of it all I was mourning my much-loved mom.

A few weeks before, a friend had asked me to join her for a long weekend in Barcelona. I was ready to cancel but my doctors told me not to change my plans, so in the middle of a depressing storm I was off to sunny Barcelona. And it really was just what the doctor ordered! In those four days I found my Self again. I regained my appetite for great food, wine, Kava, wonderful art and architecture, fun and adventure. Glowing with joy and a renewed passion for life, I returned with new energy to meet the challenges before me.

I had found my golden path again and returned to Thought Work and more. I went to Louise Hay to try to understand the whys and changes needed. Why was I creating cancer again all over the place? I knew that being aware of my thoughts was super important because wherever you place your attention expands.[1] Could thinking about the cancer in my breast add to its growth? The Law of Attraction[2] says to focus on the solution, not the problem. That meant that if I didn't want the cancer to expand and spread, I needed to stay away from tense thoughts or fears so that I wouldn't generate more cells and expansion. What kind of solution could I promote? It was to be surgically removed, which was fine with me. The most important thing was that it didn't keep growing and spreading. That gave me an idea, a kind of solution. I closed my eyes, breathing tranquilly. When I felt very calm, I visualized myself happily wrapping the small growth in a clear, impenetrable, cocoon-like wrap to prevent its expansion. I checked again and again to see that the transparent covering was hermetically sealed. I smiled at the thought of the cancer cells being flush up against the transparent wall . . . as if their noses were pushed up against a window. Whenever the growth came into my thoughts, even for a moment or two, I immediately "saw" and "reinforced" the transparent capsule. One day I "saw" them stressed out and getting upset at being so squished. I didn't want them to burst the "cocoon" open, so I "filled" the capsule with sleep-inducing gas. From that moment on I imagined them relaxed, smiling, sleeping and harmless within the transparent capsule, waiting for the doctor to take them on a trip. I didn't try to remove them with my imagination. I just wanted to prevent growth and spreading.

PREPARATION FOR SURGERY

Now it was time for some "seriously fun" mindset approaches to the surgery that would cut out the cancer. Several days before the operation I began to imagine, visualize my heart opening with complete acceptance of my doctor and the whole surgical situation. I imagined my doctor's heart and hands filling with a golden light that connected to my heart and my intentions to have a breast free of cancer with minimal aesthetic damage. My doctor had said she would reconstruct the breast as best she could for maximum aesthetics. I liked and trusted her. I also began to talk to my body and my cells. I imagined myself informing all my cells about the up-coming procedure and my total acceptance and desire for the surgery, like at a town meeting. I asked the cells close to the problem not to be afraid of the scalpel and to separate from one another in the right place for minimum scaring and maximum efficiency. And I thanked them for working with me.

I was in such a good mood when I arrived at the hospital; it wasn't surprising that I had a great roommate. She had a similar problem to mine. I had brought meditation music with me and earphones so I wouldn't bother anyone, but she liked the music so I used portable speakers attached to my smartphone to fill our room with calming, wonderful music. She was very interested in my approach, so I led her in a mediation to prepare for surgery like I had been preparing for the last days. There was a lovely comradeship – almost like summer camp.(We are still in touch.) I also brought art materials and painted a mandala to fill the hours. I was operated on the next day and released the morning after.

After the scar healed I was off to preventive radiation at a wonderful radiation centre. I brought my meditation music to fill the radiation room and everything was very pleasant. I had an amazing surprise – as soon as the radiation began I felt as if I was moving . . . floating, as if in an imaginary pool receiving a Watsu treatment. I loved it and was always sorry that the radiation treatments were so short. I had very few side effects

. . . only being very exhausted like after a long day at the beach and a few itchy spots. That's all. Maybe my love and acceptance of the treatment let the radiation leave my body without doing more harm. I like to think so.

The radiation centre also offered psychological help, which I made use of by meeting weekly with a wonderful social worker, Nina. These meetings stimulated me to do a series of watercolour paintings, which became the focus of our meetings. I have included the first and last of a series of nine paintings. The place of difficulty is very clear at the beginning of the process, as is the flow and harmony at the end. (See Plates 58 and 59.)

PRACTICES

Preparing for medical procedures

There are positive things that can be done before, during and after your various medical procedures. You can't worry and do something positive at the same time. Here are some ideas to create a calm, positive mindset to meet the challenges and situations ahead of surgery:

- Draw emotions and throw them away. If you feel a lot of stressful emotions you can always draw or paint them as a way to observe them and distance them from how you see yourself. Then you can burn the paper, tear it up, throw it in the garbage or wet it and flush it down the garbage disposal. The process can be repeated until you feel calmer.

- Your hospital may have various psychological and/or other support services, which can be very helpful.

GUIDED MEDITATION

The following two meditations enable you to visualize and have an influence over what is happening in your body and in the operating room. They also have an immediate calming effect, erasing the sense of helplessness and lack of control we feel when we aren't "in charge" or "in control".

- Guided Meditation 10 – Containing, Reducing, Erasing Tumours

- Guided Meditation 11 – Preparation for Surgery

See Chapter 21 (pages 169 and 171) for these meditations or listen to an audio recording at www.judyerel.com.

NOTES

1. The Law of Attraction: see *The Teachings of Abraham* as channelled by Esther Hicks. You can go to Appendix I for a starter and there are many books and talks that can be listened to explaining these teachings: www.Abraham-hicks.com or search on YouTube for Abraham-Hicks.

2. *Ibid.*

Chapter 19
Finding the Right Lullabies

Once the breast cancer was behind me, I began to focus on my blood problem. According to blood tests the myeloma was slowly getting stronger and stronger. I had been seeing my doctor from Tel Hashomer Hospital every month, when he told me that I would need to have chemo or biological treatments in a month or two. I was taken by surprise and knew I wanted to use all my Thought Work abilities to delay or prevent this eventuality. That was in December of 2014. Because of the amazing research and new treatments available, many cancers have become chronic, like mine. So if and when a remission turns to relapse, and it happens, I think the most important thing is not to lose your power. Meanwhile, this is what I did:

That spring I read *The Emotion Code* by Bradley Nelson because it seemed to call to me after several years of waiting on my shelf. It spoke of emotions trapped in the body's memory, which created disharmony that eventually could lead to illness and showed an easy way one could release these trapped emotions. I had started doing this process with my friend Soufa and found very interesting elements of core issues that were still trapped inside: issues such as abandonment, betrayal and low self-esteem. I used this tool to work on these emotions. I knew cancer was a smart cookie and I needed to be smarter.

To understand what was going on at another level I began to draw and paint to see what else I could find out.

Trying to be proactive I drew a mandala with gold, silver, copper and rainbow colours surrounding a purple centre of belief and intuition with a core of turquoise, copper and gold. Although that sounds utopian, something bothered me when I looked at it. (See Plate 60.)

The outer circles seemed filled with light and good energy but the core in the centre circles gave a more complex feeling – they looked muddy. I didn't understand. Some days later I made another drawing that related to the muddiness. (See Plate 61.)

I showed this drawing to a friend who also teaches and interprets mandalas and she was astonished. "This thing has taken you over, controlling your centre," she said. "All the blossoming flowers and growing plants can't get near your centre or help you." This struck a chord very deeply and I realized the myeloma had found a new and comfortable place in my core, at my expense. I had to respond unequivocally and intensely to eliminate the danger. The next drawing took almost two weeks to complete. I worked for hours each day with intensely focused concentration, intention and intuition. I started by creating my centre in the middle of the page the way I wanted it to be and then created another small circle to contain whatever is not me at my best. (See Plate 62.)

The core became very colourful, filled with hearts for self-love and acceptance, and protected by other circles filled with positive energy and love. I placed the cancer off to the side sleeping in a circle as part of a balanced yin–yang form, surrounded by copper-coloured leaves and rows of barbed growth. The leaves surrounding the yin–yang are those of zygophyllaceae plants found near the Dead Sea and other arid areas, and are thought to have cytotoxic capabilities, meaning that they can tell cells to die. They are a focus for cancer research here in Israel and all over the world. This plant and others create my garden. (See Plate 63.)

Finally, the finished garden flourished as it blossoms surrounding my being. (See Plate 64.)

When I finished that drawing, I knew I had finished for the time being. I had focused so intensely that the momentum of my thoughts focused on a solution would attract the best result. Now I had to let the healing happen.

PRACTICES

Tapping into your inner self

There are many ways your intuition tries to talk to you. One is by creating coincidences or synchronicities, so I try to keep myself open to things that catch my eye – whether it be from a book I happen to come across, a TED or YouTube talk, a lecture, something on Facebook or TV. There are so many gifts when you open yourself to a golden path. Think about it.

I usually suggest to people I work with to:

- Read *The Emotion Code* and take advantage of Bradley Nelson's way of locating and releasing trapped emotions. He created a systematic dialogue with the "body" using muscle testing (kinesiology) and a chart of emotions to uncover the trapped emotions the body is ready to release. The trapped emotions are released by swiping the body along a specific meridian using a simple magnet. The instructions are very easy to understand and his book is available on the Internet, as are Internet workshops. You can do the process yourself, with a friend or find a facilitator. I found it fascinating to see what emotions I've been hanging on to and how many levels there are to clean away.

- Express problems creatively by stating your intention and letting your creativity take you to wherever you should go. Use any media that works for you. I chose watercolour because water metaphorically represents emotions and one has less control than when using coloured pencils. As usual anything you are attracted to is good.

- Use drawing solutions because the more time and intensity you put into your "solution" drawing, the more powerful its ability to attract a solution. Like attracts like. Time spent builds momentum.

GUIDED MEDITATION 12 - EVERYDAY STANDARD CELL UPGRADE

This meditation is helpful for general balance and renewal of cells. It supports the understanding of the unity of all parts, from the smallest cell or part thereof, to the largest of the body's cooperative systems. The goal is an enlightened body with all parts working together in harmony.

You'll find the text for this guided meditation in Chapter 21 (page 172) or listen to an audio recording at www.judyerel.com.

Epilogue
Uniting the Bodymind

I am still learning who I am and who I can be . . . I'm told I look great and, of course, I believe it gladly. I practise qigong, attend a Biodanza dance class once or twice a week and continue with my weekly hiking study group. Roche Pharmaceuticals supports my guided imagery and mandala colouring activities in several major hospitals in Israel, where I use my gifts and my positivity as an inspiration to those who are where I was.

It's a done deal – an everyday challenge. I feed my body healthy foods, as I learn to continue to honour my body without manipulation or criticism. I try to meditate daily and am still on the lookout for everything on my golden path – my life's path. I enjoy my moments, hours and days as much as possible and am filled with desires for new creations and, of course, I am still working on patience. I know all is as it should be because I am still here . . . on my golden path. And I am so grateful.

Part Two
Thought Work Tool Box

"The result of an action begins with a thought."
Hebrew Proverb from *L'chadodi*,
a liturgical poem written in the Middle Ages

Chapter 20
Thought Work

Thought Work is a path connecting intention to reality using some kind of creative action. Let me define the terms for clarity sake: an intention is a thought with a purpose, aim or goal. Intentions can be conscious or unconscious, like my mother's first intention to be a "good patient and follow her doctor's lead". Thought Work's purpose is to create conscious intentions that can further your consciously chosen goals. Thoughts can be verbal or non verbal. Verbal thoughts are expressed and understood through words; nonverbal thoughts use other expressive means, like visual art, music, movement, sensing, etc. Reality can be seen in physical, emotional, mental or spiritual terms, or as the unity of all. Work is an act, action, function or activity that directs energy or exerts effort to produce a result. A creative action implies, in the narrow sense, that the imagination is used and, in the broadest sense, that the action itself produces or ignites the energy of creation. Thoughts create,[1] words create, actions create and Thought Work creates physical and non-physical outcomes.

Clear and effective intentions should be worded as positive, present tense statements[2] with positive, specific outcomes. If the intention is to get well then consider what that is for you. An effective intention might be worded: "My intention is to be on the highest point of a healing curve"; "My intention is to have high functionality with maximum comfort"; "My intention is to reach maximum healing potential easily by combining medical treatment and body–mind intelligence" or "My intention is to have a successful treatment or medical procedure" or "My intention is to fill my moments with joy and ease."

It is important to be clear and specific in your definition of healing, health or success. Intentions can be created for any situation, like "having strong, dense bones" or "cutting off the blood flow feeding a tumour". To be more than wishful thinking, Thought Work joins thought with action to focus attention, intention and will (desire) in the now moment.[3]

HOW TO BEGIN? CHOICE IS POWER.
CONSCIOUS CHOOSING EMPOWERS CONSCIOUSLY.

Serious illness is a wakeup call. It shouts that something has missed our attention big time. When you get a wakeup call, it's time to wake up. It's time to become aware of both conscious and unconscious choices that have been made. It's time to look boldly at the kind of life you want; the kind of life you live; what thoughts occupy your attention; what you fear and what you are sure of; what feels good and what feels bad. It's time to consider the significance of where and what kind of imbalance is involved and which conscious choices can bring you joy and balance.

Choosing consciously to engage and assume responsibility (the ability to respond) is a huge step and an enormous opportunity for personal growth. It places you in an active mode rather than a passive one. Everything flows from this decision.

You might want to go through it alone, with help from family, friends, books, recordings or the Internet; you might look for someone to coach you throughout or just for a while, or any combination of the above. The important thing is to have a sense of trust in yourself and your guidance, human or otherwise. As for guidance, it is said when the student is ready a teacher appears. With today's technology the world is wherever you are and everything is possible.

You need not know all the answers or all the questions. Just begin by choosing to engage and use the following "what to dos" to guide you.

- **Examine your reality:** Look at the physical issues you face, how you cope emotionally, and what feelings, attitudes and behaviour patterns appear. Serious situations provide unique opportunities and strong motivation for change and empowerment. Examine what you like about yourself and your life, as well as what you don't like. This is where conscious engagement begins.

- **Decide what you want to release and find ways to let go:** After examining your reality, create a list of what you would like to change or release. A clear agenda helps guide thinking and begins with recognizing what supports and what hinders your real goals.[4] Everything has meaning and can be helpful.

- **Fill your inner space consciously:** When unwanted cells are released through medications, treatments, surgery, creative expression and meditation, etc. you have a chance to refill that space. What do you want to fill this "emptiness" with? Take the opportunity to fill "empty space" consciously. I always choose something that relates to joy.

- **Transform specific problems:** Specific issues can be attended to, zoomed in on and addressed. "The result of action begins with thought",[5] so what thoughts support your desired results? Begin from what is and aim for your best-case scenario. Let thought and creative expression release, erase, refill, dissolve, reshape, renew, redo, rebuild, redesign[6] . . . to plant the seeds of transformation.

- **Balance the whole you:** All cells, healthy and problematic, are aware of and affected by medications, drugs, treatments, stress, diet and emotions like joy, worry and anxiety. Various techniques to create balance support the wellbeing of the whole and its parts and can ease physical, emotional and energetic strain.

- **Maintain your gain:** Healthy eating habits and regular physical activity support general health. Now add positive mindsets and intention-based actions to help maintain mind–body balance. Like musical instruments tuning up before a performance, the body and its parts can be tuned to perform with greater inner harmony. Fine-tuning, rebalance, awareness and intention-based actions can encourage wellness and discourage imbalance and the reoccurrence of illness.

THOUGHT WORK CREATIVE TOOLBOX

These basic tools can be mixed and matched: mindful breathing, guided imagery, meditation, active gratitude, focused conscious attention, journaling, nonverbal creative expression and physical activity all add to the desired outcome. These tools are not new, but their application to promoting health, wellbeing and manifesting intentions is part of a new, proactive, empowered way of being in the world. They belong to the new paradigm as the basis of the Self united to heal, where all levels of being – physical, emotional, mental and spiritual – work in concert. Here is a list and short description of basic tools used in the first part of this book:

MINDFUL BREATH

Mindful breathing is a powerful, nonverbal tool available any time, anywhere. Simply breathe while placing your attention on every moment of the in-breath, the out-breath and the spaces in between. As your attention is filled by your breath, there is less and less space for other thoughts and sensations. This is the way mindful breathing quiets mental noise. It can be used to calm and quiet yourself or as the first step for other Thought Work tools like meditation, guided imagery, journaling and creative expression. Mindful breathing is an easy way to enter the here and now. I always tell first timers that it is natural for stray thoughts to enter your mind. If that happens just notice and, with no more ado, turn your attention back to breathing the in-breath . . . the out-breath . . . the spaces in between in the present moment.

ACTIVE GRATITUDE OR THANKFULNESS

Gratitude is a state of mind and a powerful creative tool. The act of enumerating what you are grateful for (people, qualities, relationships, things, situations, etc.) and focusing on feeling the gratitude[7] is a wonderful way to switch mental balance from negative to positive. When we fill ourselves with gratitude, the immediate result is a drop in hopelessness, helplessness and victimhood. The effect is far reaching, joy enhancing, boosts mental, emotional and physical resilience and puts you in tune to attract positive things into your life. The gratitude tool is always beneficial: wonderful in the morning as you begin your day, exquisite before sleep as you end it and lovely any time in between. For starters you can be grateful to yourself for remembering to be grateful and then focus on the feeling of being grateful.

GUIDED IMAGERY MEDITATION[8] OR GUIDED IMAGERY

This technique directs thoughts and guides a meditative process that engages the imagination to feel, intend, visualize and/or experience. As previously mentioned, your thoughts flood your body with chemical messages and your body reacts. A meditative state enhances the body–mind connection influencing wherever your imagination leads. You can guide yourself or be guided by an instructor, tapes or scripts to help you through the process. It is very important to know that people "imagine", "see" and "envision" differently. Some people see full-blown movies; some only images; some see nothing, but "know"; others sense or feel sensations in their bodies and still others have a little of this and a little of that. Some people "get it" right away and some don't. No one way is more effective or better than another.

This tool can be used for:

- General relaxation
- Cleansing and energizing
- Releasing negative emotions or energy
- Filling a void with whatever you choose
- Influencing biological processes at the atomic, cellular and tissue level
- Creating personalized visualizations to balance and maintain inner harmony

And anything else you can think of.

CONSCIOUS ATTENTION

The idea that "you are not in control of thoughts that travel through your head, but you are in control of the ones that stay there" is almost a cliché. Loving, happy thoughts create one kind of chemical reaction in the body while depressing, stressful or frightening thoughts create another. There are physical consequences to the thoughts we pay attention to. What is on our minds (our attention) or on our tongues (our words) interacts to colour how we perceive the world and create our internal physical environment. This makes the ability to focus attention consciously an immensely powerful tool worth developing.

One important aspect is paying attention to words we use to describe reality. Think of the different possibilities, approaches and scenarios that open or close when a situation is described as: difficult or complex or a "problem", a "misfortune", a "challenge" or a "tragedy". Although each may have some truth, which is the most empowering? What potentials are fostered with each choice? Which holds the highest possibility for positive development?

JOURNALING

Journaling is writing from an uncensored, personal point of view. It's a way to record conversations with yourself and to express semiconscious thoughts. You can use a special journal, a plain notebook, single sheets of paper or a computer. Journaling provides a safe place to repeat yourself, vent, exaggerate, blame or dwell in self-pity. If you write it, it evidently needs to be expressed. Journaling means writing, not necessarily reading and rereading, showing others nor giving weight to what's written. By expressing on paper we can see our thoughts as separate from ourselves. Thoughts reflect what is inside. Some reflect positive aspects, others negative. You can do what you wish with the written pages – even burn them joyously. The process, the here and now doing, is important, not the result. Here are some forms and objectives.

AUTOMATIC WRITING

This is simply writing whatever comes to mind and is good for general release or when you want to open a conversation with your inner self. You may feel a strong need to write, which makes things easier. But if you don't know how to begin . . . just write your thoughts, even if that means writing "what shall I write, what shall I write" . . . until something else comes. I sometimes use a form of automatic writing in which I write questions and then write whatever answers pop into my head as the response.

31: *Healing and Gratitude Mandala,*
watercolour and ink

32: *Healing and Gratitude Mandala,*
watercolour and ink

33: *Healing and Gratitude Mandala,*
watercolour and ink

34: *Healing and Gratitude Mandala,*
watercolour and ink

35: *Healing and Gratitude Mandala*, watercolour and ink

36: *Purpleness and Smiles*,
watercolour and ink

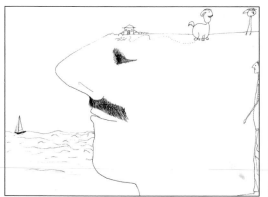

37: A silly drawing using tiny purple drips
for hats

38: *More Smiles to Fill My Cells*, ink

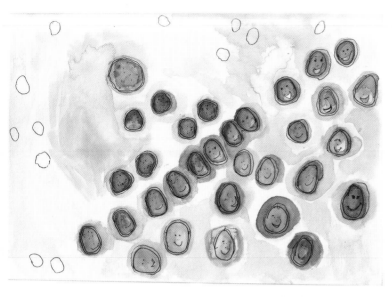

39: *Happy Harvest*,
watercolour

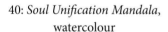

40: *Soul Unification Mandala*,
watercolour

41: *Client Choosing Feelings and Thoughts to Be
Released During the Transplant*,
watercolour and coloured pencils

42: *Client Choosing Feelings to Flourish*,
watercolour and coloured pencils

43: *Client Filling Body and Stem Cells with Joy*, coloured pencils

44: *Client Affirmations and Mandala to be Completed in the Hospital*, pencil and coloured pencils

45: *I Am Worthy of a Healthy Body Mandala 1*, pencil

46: *I Am Worthy of a Healthy Body Mandala 3*, mixed media

47: Willpower and moments of strength

48: Joy and satisfaction

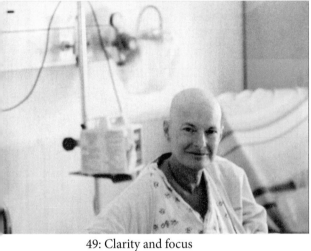

49: Clarity and focus

50: The wise old sage

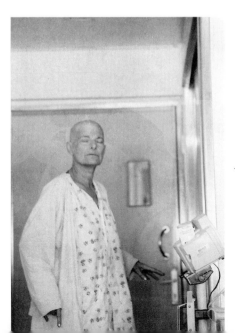

51:
Weakness and frailty

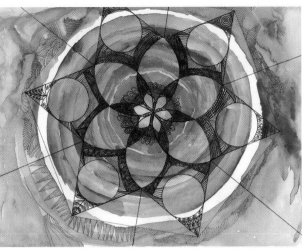

52: *Healing Mandala*, watercolour and ink

53: *Healing and Growth Mandala*,
watercolour and ink

54: *New Growth Mandala*, watercolour and ink

55: *Growth and Healing in All Directions*,
watercolour and coloured pencils

56: Desert shadows

58: *Radiation 1*, watercolour, pencil, ink

57: Hiking the wadi

59: *Radiation 9*, watercolour

60: *Rainbow Mandala*, mixed media

61: *The Takeover*, watercolour and ink

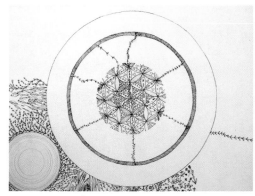

62: *Setting the New Scene*,
pencil and ink

63: *Composing the Lullaby*,
pencil and watercolour

64: *Singing the Lullaby*, mixed media

WRITTEN OBSERVATIONS

When you write observations you watch situations from a distance, which helps you look at your experiences and your feelings about them. This can be especially helpful when a lot is going on because you can deal with one thing at a time and digest things bit by bit.

BRAINSTORMING

When you need to seriously consider complex situations, brainstorming encourages writing down ideas – or parts of ideas, asking questions, compiling purposeful to-do lists or dealing with them without judgement. Whether the ideas are good or bad is considered later. Sometimes writing down less-valuable ideas will lead you to finding the more profound ones. Here are some brainstormable issues:

- What do you want to release from your life and what do you want to create and flourish?
- Attitudes, fears and feelings you have relating to medical treatments
- Issues you are dealing with
- Memories connecting the present with the past
- Preparations to support various medical procedures
- Positive affirmations that could be beneficial.

FOLLOW-UPS

Follow-ups help decode what your body and life are telling you by organizing and gathering together brainstormed ideas and journaled materials. It's fascinating to see how we are guided by inner wisdom. It may be important to read and reread some things to let the meaning sink in and understand connections. If you consult others, as I did by using Louise Hay's books, be sure to trust yourself and your own gut feelings when you examine anyone else's suggestions. If it doesn't feel right for you, it probably isn't. Examining the significance of what you are facing can help you uncover personal behaviour patterns and reveal what you need to be released or strengthened. Trust your gut.

COMMITMENT, FOCUS AND ENHANCING MOTIVATION

Your focus, commitment and motivation will not always be the same. I found that I received an amazing boost each time I formally engaged others in "conversation" through my email updates and invitations because they served as clear opportunities to re-declare my intentions and choices to focus the support I wanted from others and myself.

Then I used Gadi's creatorship pages and life–work chart to help organize and focus my time as I reported to him. You can use state-of-the-art social media venues or more intimate means. What is common to all is that they involve someone else's presence in the process – virtual or real – and your declaration and commitment. The number of people you share with isn't important, what matters is the strength the process gives you. Your commitment to your healing path renews your oaths to yourself and enables others to support you in the way you choose.

CREATIVE EXPRESSION

Expressive activity can be used to articulate, release and empower change. This nonverbal "doing" creates balance, increases calm and provides quality time enjoyment. When you focus your attention on what you are doing, you mindfully enter the here and now. Then the mind's chatter stops and fosters a state of inner quiet where self-healing thrives. You'll find that not being aware of time passing will help you know which creative activities will put you in the "zone"; for example: drawing, painting, sculpting, mixed media, playing an instrument, singing, dancing, movement, cooking, washing dishes, gardening, sports, making practical things, etc. Adding intentions to your activity supports your purpose. That said, I focus on drawing and painting because I love it, it can be done in most physical conditions, materials are lightweight and easily accessible (a pencil or pen and paper are the minimum) and you don't have to be an artist to express yourself to yourself. If you prefer other means of expression – go for it.

Expressing emotions, pain and/or positive or negative feelings by drawing or painting lines, shapes, colours (sculpting with das, modelling dough or clay, food, etc.). Remember, the process is what is important . . . not the final result. In addition to the actual doing, visualizing the process with meaning or significance enhances the creative power of the activity. The result of your efforts can be thought of as seeds planted to become a new now, or as something to be empowered or released from your body or your life.

COMMUNICATING WITH YOUR UNCONSCIOUS AND SEMICONSCIOUS

Like "automatic writing", intuitive drawing and doodling awakens an inner dialogue. Let your hand lead you to colours, shapes, lines, images and then "play with them". Note how you feel regarding your choices. Every step is a creative choice, whether you use white paper, black or coloured paper backgrounds, a compass, ruler or intuitive lines; work from the centre, from the edges, on the whole paper or within various sections. You might choose to begin by drawing a circular format to contain what is within or start by placing a dot, line, shape or image on a blank sheet of paper and go where it leads you. Your next choice will be part of the dialogue between what is on the page and what is about to be added to it. Enjoy.

TRANSFORMATIONAL DRAWING

This is based on a conscious intention to change or transform something in your present to something else. It can be used to: fill empty spaces with what you want in your body, your life or your world; fix something broken, imbalanced or weakened; nurture some things or eliminate others. In addition, transformational drawings often clarify ideas for visualizations, which can be used as you work or after the drawings are finished.

MANDALA DRAWINGS

Creating mandalas is a meditation in itself – a doorway to the soul. Jung brought mandala drawing to the fore as a therapeutic path to the Self and considered the mandala as an archetype of the Self and the path to the Self, which he called "individuation". Today it is considered an art therapy technique that intuitively strives towards balance and harmony by unifying opposites. This activity is amazingly calming and places the doer in a tranquil place of renewal. Sometimes working on geometric patterns provides the balance, comfort and platform needed; other times recognizable images, abstract designs or just doodles are appropriate. Of course combinations are fine too. For Thought Work purposes, the rule is there are no rules – just do what feels right at the moment. While drawing you may want to jot down the thoughts and feelings that arise in a journal, on the back of the paper or include words in the mandala itself. You can use ready-made designs (the Internet is filled with them) or create your own mandalas based on a circle[9] or just work free-form. Directions to create some basic geometric mandala designs can be found in Chapter 23, pages 182–187.

BEING CREATIVE WITH ANY PHYSICAL EXPRESSIONS

Whether sculpting mashed potatoes into a healed bone and eating the health; weeding a garden of weeds that represent anger or cancer cells and patting the hole left in the ground to fill it with love and health; dancing expressively or mindfully; walking while imagining your body getting stronger with each step; or cleansing yourself inside and out in the shower – any act can be turned into a tool for creative expressions when accompanied by intention. If you want to add a shamanic touch, you can always plant words, drawings or symbolic seeds in the earth, symbolizing what you want to flourish, and burn and bury symbols of what you want to be rid of.

PHYSICAL ACTIVITY

There are many options, depending on what you are able to do (check with your doctor) and love to do. Whatever you do, you can add the intention of improving your health with each movement, step and practice. There are so many physical activities from running, bicycling to dancing. Find what you like or try something new. Here are some examples of physical activities I've used:

Watsu, hydrotherapy, walking, bone-building exercises, pilates, the Feldenkrais method, yoga, Iyengar yoga, laughing yoga, tai chi, qigong and of course dancing (Biodanza). Qigong especially has special healing trainings that are cancer specific, e.g. Shen Zhen Healing Gong under Master Li Junfeng (http://shengzhen.org) or the healing qigong practices of Master Mingtong Gu (www.chicenter.com) who uses sound healing and movement. Both can be done sitting. Mingtong brought his qigong practices from the largest qigong hospital in China to the West. Both are on YouTube and have DVDs that can be purchased. I do both and love it.

WHEN IS A GOOD TIME FOR THOUGHT WORK?

Basically whenever is perfect. Each of the stages below has its way to relate to the various Thought Work possibilities. The moment you consciously decide to do a Thought Work activity, no matter what you do, you are declaring to yourself that you are in a proactive mindset. You know you are using your thoughts and actions for a purpose.

- **Pre diagnosis:** Instead of worrying, do some Thought Work to express the tension or release feelings behind the problem and to create your best solution.

- **Before treatment:** Thought Work preparations can be empowering for radiation, chemo, surgery and other procedures.

- **During treatments:** Use Thought Work activities to support goals during hospitalizations.

- **After-treatment activities:** Use Thought Work to further treatment goals, deal with side effects and fill boring waiting room time.

- **Focusing on specific needs:** Use Thought Work to strengthen, erase, rewire, remodel and/or rebuild specific situations.

- **Focusing on general needs:** Use Thought Work to talk to your cells, tissues and genes to balance your whole body.

- **To address relapses:** Use Thought Work for on-going care, maintenance, balance and fine-tuning.

NOTES

1. In her bestselling book *The Intention Experiment*, Lynne McTaggart (2007) presents a fascinating array of methodologically tight, evidence-based, cutting-edge scientific experiments revealing the influence of thought on physicality. Her discussion helped me understand what I did in more scientific terms and how creative activity based on clear, detailed intention facilitates the direction and quality of change. Her findings claim that the power of intention is best mobilized when combined with strong desire, concentration, detailed specifics and action in the now moment. See www.Theintentionexperiment.com.

2. Why a positive statement? It has been shown that the mind does not recognize negatives. If I say "Don't think of a pink elephant!", what pops into your mind? A pink elephant. So If I say I want no pain . . . somehow the pain scale is still part of my attention. If you intend "to want to be healthy", that can also be problematic. That intention may be calling in the wanting of health and not the health itself. For clarity's sake I would say "My intention is to be healthy . . . or I am healthy." Why present tense? Because that is the only time frame in which creation takes place. The past is over; the future isn't here yet. Present tense statements bring what we want into the now – where we can live it – or plant it as a seed to bloom in the future.

3. Ekhardt Tolle, *The Power of Now*. Vancouver, Canada: Namaste Publishing, 1999.

4. For example, my agenda became creating a life of love, creativity, health and joy and releasing everything that did not promote it.

5. Hebrew proverb from *L'chadodi*, a liturgical poem written in the Middle Ages.

6. My spine drawings and kidney slices in Part I are examples of working on specific problems.

7. You can also breathe in this gratitude; envision your whole body filling with gratitude.

8. The *Encarta Dictionary* in Microsoft Word defines meditation as: "1. the emptying of the mind of thoughts, or the concentration of the mind on one thing, in order to aid mental or spiritual development, relaxation or contemplation. 2. The act of thinking about something carefully, calmly, seriously, and for some time, or an instance of such thinking."

9. I say based on a circle because squaring the circle and perfect geometric shapes are based on and derived from the circle and are also considered mandalas.

Chapter 21
Guided Meditations

There are many ways to meditate. I am open to what makes me relaxed. There is no particular body position I consider "correct" for meditation. You may choose to meditate sitting with your feet touching the floor, sitting cross-legged (or yoga style), or lying down or whatever . . . as long as you are comfortable. If you are not sitting yoga style it is best not to cross your legs. There are also many different hand positions. Basically each has its own meaning and all are good. My personal favourite is to relaxingly leave my palms open to receive whatever gifts the meditation may bring. For me it is a declaration of choosing to receive and focusing on myself. The most important thing is to be relaxed and comfortable, so do what feels good to you at the time.

Please know that distracting thoughts may enter your mind while you are meditating. It happens to everyone, so don't be frustrated. When you notice that you are in the midst of a distraction, be happy that you noticed and then return to the meditation by focusing on your breathing once again.

Another important thing to know is that different people "see" differently. Some "know", some "feel", some "visually experience" a movie or scene, others just colours, some "hear" and some "sense" the experience. Each way is good and has its benefits.

A recording of each of the following guided meditations can be accessed on my website www.judyerel.com.

GUIDED MEDITATION 1: CALM, LIGHT AND JOY

Sit or lie down in a comfortable position with the palm of your hands facing upwards, declaring your readiness and openness to receive. Now gently close your eyes . . . and place your attention on your breathing . . . be with the breathing process as you breathe in . . . and breathe out. As you inhale . . . and exhale . . . inhale and . . . exhale. Be aware of the speed of your breathing . . . is it fast or slow? Is your breathing shallow or deep?

Whatever it is . . . is just fine . . . the focus of your attention and observation is what is important. This is what is called mindful breathing . . . being aware . . . of the breath at each present moment.

Now imagine that you are observing yourself in a nature movie . . . and imagine that with the air you breathe . . . you are also breathing in light . . . light particles . . . light waves . . . coming from the sun . . . from the universe . . . from God . . . Jesus . . . Allah . . . Elohim, from the Creative Source of everything.

As the light enters your face . . . and head . . . you sense a pleasant calm and quiet . . . in your mind . . . your thoughts. The light begins to fill your insides . . . your tissues . . . your cells . . . your molecules . . . even the atoms that make up your physical body. The light fills your throat and the back of your neck . . . gently dispersing tension . . . now your shoulders and arms fill with light . . . that flows all the way down to your fingertips . . . imagine relaxing tensions . . . aches . . . and distractions . . . Now your torso fills with light . . . breathe in rays of light to fill each cell . . . in your chest and ribs . . . your spine . . . your lungs, each cell in each of your internal organs . . . Each cell is nourished . . . with oxygen . . . and light. See the light move downwards . . . into your thighs . . . your knees . . . your shins . . . your ankles . . . your feet and toes . . . If there is a place in your body that still feels tense or achy, breathe into it . . . to flood it with more light. Now imagine the light continuing through your feet . . . flowing downwards . . . until it reaches the centre of our Earth.

Imagine that you have become like a glowing pearl . . . connecting Heaven and Earth. What a wonderful, joyous place to be. The light connecting Heaven and Earth is made of energy . . . energy of love and joy.

Imagine yourself being blessed with love . . . and joy . . . as trillions of microscopic smileys ☺ gather around your feet. There are yellow smileys smiling . . . and smileys of self-love with hearts for eyes . . . and kissing smileys with a heart for lips. Imagine the smileys excitedly waiting for an invitation to enter your body . . . and when you say "yes" in your heart . . . they enter . . . jumping over one another, giggling . . . to find a cell to fill with joy and love. Laughingly they begin filling the skin cells of your feet . . . then they move into your arteries . . . and veins . . . they enter your blood cells . . . they enter your lymphatic cells . . . they jump into your nerve cells . . . your bone cells . . . your muscles cells . . . fat cells . . . cartilage . . . the connective tissue cells connecting bones to bones . . .

muscles to bones . . . muscles to muscles. When your feet are filled with smiles and love . . . the smileys continue running up your shins filling each cell . . . up to your knees . . . then up into each cell of your thighs . . . and into your torso. Each cell in your pelvis and reproductive organs fills with smileys . . . your entire digestive system fills with smileys . . . all of your bones . . . all the internal organs . . . your liver . . . pancreas . . . gall bladder . . . bladder . . . kidneys . . . spleen . . . all the cells in your organs up to your waist . . . into your vertebrae cells . . . your lung cells . . . heart cells . . . breast cells . . . chest cells . . . your fingers to your arms . . . your shoulders . . . all the cells up to your throat and the back of the neck fill with smileys . . . they continue to fill the cells in your head . . . and face . . . into your brain . . . and your thoughts . . . to help you think good loving thoughts . . . your eyes, ears and nose from within fill with smileys to sense the joy and the love. Then your mouth fills with smileys . . . your gums . . . teeth . . . tongue . . . and your lips. Each cell in your body now vibrates at the vibration of love . . . self-love . . . and joy.

You may remain in this loving state for as long as you wish. When you wish to awaken gently move your fingers . . . your toes . . . and slowly open your eyes with a huge smile on your face.

GUIDED MEDITATION 2: UNITING WITH INTENTIONS

Before you begin the meditation, I invite you to formulate an intention or two using only positive, present tense sentences. Read over the intentions or decisions that you want to work with. What is the desire behind your intention? Simplify and be exacting with your words. In this meditation I shall use the desire for good health and the intention of having my cells create harmony and cooperation within my body. You may use any other desire or intention you choose.

Sit or lie down in a comfortable position with the palm of your hands facing upwards, declaring your readiness and openness to receive . . . Gently close your eyes . . . place your attention on your breathing . . . It is time to enter the quiet . . .

Take three deep cleansing breaths . . . inhaling through your nose and exhaling through your mouth . . . leaving a few moments between inhales and exhales. As you take your first breath . . . inhale through your nose . . . Imagine that with the air . . . you are also breathing in light, balance and joy. Hold your breath for a moment . . . and then slowly exhale through your mouth. Know that as you release the air you also release the shadows . . . tension or heaviness you may be holding on to. Take your second deep breath . . . again inhaling the air through your nose along with light, love and acceptance. After you hold your breath . . . purposely exhale any tension . . . worries . . . negative thoughts. Repeat this once more . . . deeply inhale light . . . ease . . . and purity . . . hold . . . and then exhale releasing tension . . . difficulty and darkness. Feel yourself as energized . . . cleansed . . . and ready.

Now imagine a small ball of light . . . glowing inside you . . . in the area of your solar plexus . . . just below the centre of your rib cage and diaphragm. This is the light of desire. Since the intensity of light . . . reflects the intensity of your desires. And the strength of your desires mobilizes the power of your intentions . . . Imagine this ball of light . . . of desire . . . filling with willpower . . . focus . . . and aspirations as you watch it . . . and see it begin to grow . . . and glow even more intensely. As the glowing light grows . . . and glows . . . its spiral motion fills your chest cavity . . . and your abdomen. As it fills with more desire . . . focus . . . willpower . . . the glowing light expands its spiral to shine through your neck . . . shoulders . . . arms . . . thighs . . . knees . . . your head . . . and hair . . . your shins . . . and feet . . . Your whole body is now engulfed in this ball of desire . . . and you glow. You glow intensely . . .

This light of desire radiates deeply inwards . . . touching each cell in your body.

Imagine your cells smiling and enjoying the warming, loving glow. They are touched by the desire for . . . Good Health . . . Love . . . Abundance . . . Wellbeing . . . whatever you choose.

When the desire is intense enough . . . an intention can begin to flow . . . to become . . . like a glowing . . . growing flame that spirals out from your centre . . . your essence. The intention for all the cells of the body to work in harmony to reach a state of abundant health. Harmonious wellbeing . . . fills each cell the light touches. The message expands on a circular path . . . enveloping each cell of your entire body. You can see the spiralling light circling out from your centre . . . expanding to all parts of your torso and arms . . . touching your neck and your legs . . . your face and head and your ankles and feet.

Yes! Feel your body, mind and soul . . . unified in balanced cooperation . . . filled with the light of intention. Know that the manifestation of your intention is powered by the strength of your positive clear desires . . . intentions and actions. Repeat your intention to yourself or out loud, "Each cell in my body works in harmony to reach a state of wonderful, abundant health . . . Each day, each cell fills with joy and focus to fulfil this intention . . . Imagine your cells joyful . . . focused . . . creating the harmony that reduces the power and disharmony of illness . . . See yourself in your mind's eye happy . . . enjoying life . . . filled with gratitude for all the gifts of health you can imagine.

You may remain with this feeling of having your being filled with empowerment . . . for as long as you wish . . . Then to exit the meditative state . . . gently move your fingers . . . and your toes . . . and open your eyes gently with a huge smile on your face and a sense of total balance in your heart.

GUIDED MEDITATION 3: CHE-MOTHER-APY

Before you begin the meditation, it's good to remember that chemotherapy – or che-mother-apy can be thought of as mother energy therapy and biological treatments can be thought of as life therapies (bio = life). Words reflect attitudes making the treatment a bit more palatable. It is good to do this guided meditation before, during and/or after your treatment.

Sit or lay down in a comfortable position with the palms of your hands facing upwards . . . declaring your readiness and openness to receive. Go into the quiet . . . mindfully. Gently close your eyes . . . and place your attention on your breathing . . . notice as you breathe in . . . and breathe out . . . as you inhale . . . and exhale . . . inhale and . . . exhale. Be aware of the speed of your breathing . . . is it fast? . . . or is it slow? . . . Is your breathing shallow? . . . or is your breathing deep? Whatever it is . . . is just fine . . . the focus of your attention . . . and observation is what is important. You are breathing mindfully . . . you are aware . . . of your breath at each present moment. You are calm . . . and at peace.

When you feel yourself "in the quiet" . . . imagine yourself – the CEO of your body . . . talking quietly to the conscious awareness . . . of each cell in your body . . . let all your cells know . . . that you have chosen to have this treatment . . . and the che-mother-apy or life therapy is entering your body with your approval. Tell the chemotherapy or biotherapy molecules that they are welcome to do their magic and then may leave your body gracefully and easily . . . causing the least disturbance possible . . . Tell your cells to let any imbalance go . . . easily . . .

Now . . . imagine light entering your body . . . with each breath . . . filling your face . . . head . . . neck . . . the back of the neck . . . releasing any tension and discomfort . . . The light enters your shoulders and arms . . . down to your finger tips . . . The light fills your chest . . . back . . . Your lungs fill with light . . . your heart fills with light . . . your vertebra, spine, ribs . . . Now every cell in your body and organs down to your waist . . . fills with light . . . The light flows down to your pelvis. Your whole digestive system and all the organs that surround it fill with light . . . so you can digest your food better . . . taking what is good for you and releasing the rest. So you can digest your emotions better . . . keeping what supports healing and releasing the rest . . . digesting situations better . . . so you can keep what supports you and release the rest.

Now your legs fill with light from your thighs to the tips of your toes. The light continues flowing down into the floor . . . and goes down to the bottom level of wherever you are . . . until it reaches deep into the earth. Now you are like a pearl filled with light connecting Heaven and Earth . . . What a lovely place to be . . . a place filled with love.

At the molecular level . . . the light enhances the harmony . . . and consciousness of your healthy cells . . . Healthy cells love the light . . . but cancer cells hate this harmony . . . and hate the light. They start moving around, looking for a way out of their discomfort . . .

Now imagine that a large criss-cross web of copper light the width of your whole body is above your head . . . This net will filter the energy of each cell . . . the copper strands of light magnetically pull anything that is not harmonious into its web . . . Like a coffee press filter pushing the coffee grains downwards . . . the particles, cells . . . memories . . . and thoughts that don't support health and joy will be collected and filtered out of your body.

Imagine the copper light filter above your head . . . the light filter moves downwards to the top of your head . . . through your head, collecting microscopic negative thoughts, energies, worries, memories. The filter presses downwards, reaching your eye level . . .

your chin . . . collecting all the disharmony down to your throat . . . your shoulders . . . chest . . . arms . . . to your waist . . . down through your digestive system . . . to your reproductive system . . . and your pelvis . . . through to your legs . . . knees . . . ankles . . . feet and toes . . . The filter continues down through the floor . . . all the way into the ground . . . where the energy and granules disintegrate into the earth.

Ahhhh . . . breathe deeply . . . Feel the lightness of vacant space where disease and disharmony have been released. Now we can fill these spaces with something positive . . . something we choose.

Let's fill these empty spaces with wonderful smileys ☺ . . . smileys with hearts for eyes . . . smileys with lips kissing with love . . . flowers and joy. Imagine trillions of yellow microscopic smileys gathered around your feet. Imagine calling to the smileys to enter your body . . . telling them to find all the empty spaces . . . that were once filled with negativity, disharmony and cancer . . . As they enter your feet . . . they jump over one another . . . to find a place to fill with joy . . . and love . . . Laughingly . . . they begin filling the skin cells of your feet . . . then they move into your arteries . . . and veins . . . they enter your blood cells . . . they enter your lymphatic cells . . . they jump into your nerve cells . . . your bone cells . . . your muscles cells . . . fat cells . . . connective tissue cells . . . The smileys continue running up your body . . . filling each place cleaned out by the chemotherapy and your own body-mind wisdom. They fill your legs and enter your torso . . . Filling all empty spaces . . . When they reach the area where you have cancer . . . they fill each molecule and each atom with smileys, love and joy. When your smileys have filled each available space from your pelvis to your waist . . . to your diaphragm . . . all your organs . . . your liver, kidneys, spleen, gallbladder, pancreas . . . your lungs, heart, breasts, all the lymph nodes . . . they continue up into your neck . . . The smileys enter each cell in your head . . . and flow into your brain . . . and your thoughts . . . your eyes, ears and nose from within fill with smileys to sense the joy and the love . . . Then your mouth fills with smileys . . . your gums . . . teeth . . . tongue . . . and your lips . . . Each cell in your body now vibrates at the vibration of love . . . self-love . . . and joy.

You may remain in the quiet for as long as you wish . . . and then gently open your eyes with a huge smile on your face.

GUIDED MEDITATION 4: SEA OF LIGHT

Find your comfortable position for meditation and place the palms of your hands facing upwards . . . declaring your readiness and openness to receive . . . Go into the quiet . . . mindfully . . . by gently closing your eyes . . . with your attention on your breathing . . . Observe your breath as you breathe in . . . and breathe out . . . as you inhale . . . and exhale . . . inhale and . . . exhale.

Feel a sense of quiet . . . and calm . . . imagine that you are walking . . . on a very special glowing path . . . a pathway of diamond dust granules . . . as soft as a wonderful sandy white beach . . . You feel the granules between your toes . . . as you walk barefoot . . . through this exotic landscape . . . The path ends at the mouth of a strange cave . . . This cave is filled with light, not darkness . . . As you enter . . . you see the walls of the cave glisten and sparkle . . . they are made of stunning multi-coloured crystals . . . You walk down the entrance hallway of the cave . . . until there is a turn to the left . . . into even more light . . . You keep walking until you enter a huge underground space that glows with light so bright that you can hardly see. When your eyes adjust a bit, you see what looks to be an underground lake . . . but instead of regular water it looks like liquid light. You look down at your bare feet . . . walking in the diamond dust as it comes to the shoreline of the liquid light sea . . . that glows stronger than the sunniest day. Truly . . . a pool of light . . . a sea of glowing blessings.

With joy you begin to enter the pool of light . . . You take a step with one foot . . . and then the other . . . You imagine the liquid light surrounding the skin of your feet . . . Now imagine the liquid light flowing deeper into your feet . . . filling each foot inside and out with its glow . . . Every cell . . . every molecule of your feet begin to vibrate with light energy . . . Take another two steps forward and your ankles fill with light. You can imagine the light energy moving . . . flowing . . . as you take another step . . . and another . . . You move deeper into the pool of light . . . slowly . . . enjoying the sensations of this energy . . . love energy . . . Now feel the light entering your shins . . . and with more steps deeper into the light . . . you feel your knees . . . and your thighs become "enlightened" . . . glowing . . . You continue walking deeper and deeper and feel your body fill with light up to your belly button . . . up to your waist. All your internal organs and systems are filling with light as your hands, arms and chest allow the sea of light . . . to flow through it. As you go deeper and deeper your throat . . . neck . . . head . . . and face fill with light . . . Soon you find your entire head in the pool of light . . . yet you can breathe easily . . . you keep walking forward . . . deeper and deeper until you are completely submerged . . . filling with light energy. You float in the sea of light . . . completely immersed in light energy . . . love energy . . . in harmony with the universe . . . feeling totally whole . . . totally cleansed . . . totally you. You can see your desires and intentions be enhanced before your very eyes.

You feel nourished . . . The light scans everything from the tip of your head, your brain, your throat . . . your lungs . . . your heart . . . your whole body. When the light feels something is needed it . . . renews and restores what is needed. Anything that can be released is dissolved and disintegrates. Let yourself feel blessed and filled with gratitude.

When it is time to leave, you swim through the liquid light. When you are close to the shore . . . stand up . . . and walk slowly out of the pool of light. Your body is glowing intensely . . . your head peeps out of the pool . . . your neck and shoulders are above the "sea of light" . . . Slowly other parts of your body peak above the pool . . . your chest . . . up to your waist . . . your pelvis . . . your thighs . . . your knees . . . your feet . . . Finally when you step out of the pool of light and on to the shore of diamond dust . . . you see your entire body is still glowing vibrantly. You look down at your footprints in the diamond dust. They too are glowing. You continue walking . . . and see other glowing footprints in the diamond dust . . . You know that whoever walks in your footsteps will be gifted with the glow of your light . . . as you will be gifted with the light of others.

The feeling of unity . . . of connection . . . of your glowing body and of the connection we all have for each other . . . go with you as you leave the wonderful cave of light . . .

Feel the power of enlightenment in each molecule of your body . . . And when you are ready . . . Slowly open your eyes . . . with a big smile on your face.

GUIDED MEDITATION 5: CHE-MOTHER-APY FAREWELL PARTY

Find your comfortable position for meditation . . . and place the palms of your hands facing upwards . . . declaring your readiness and openness to receive . . . Go into the quiet

. . . mindfully . . . by gently closing your eyes . . . with your attention on your breathing . . . observe your breath as you breathe in . . . and breathe out . . . as you inhale . . . and exhale . . . inhale and . . . exhale.

When you feel a sense of quiet . . . and calm . . . imagine that you are surrounded by everyone you love . . . and that loves you . . . from your present . . . from the past . . . even people who no longer are alive . . . Imagine where you are . . . It may be outside in nature . . . at the beach . . . or in a lovely celebration hall. Everyone you want to participate joins in spirit to support your celebrations.

You truly know . . . in your soul . . . that you want your body . . . and life to reflect the joy, health . . . love . . . and passion for life . . . that you deserve. A strong decision is made . . . and YES it is indeed a time for celebration . . . Your body unites with the desires of your mind . . . and heart . . . to support the transformation of dis-ease and disharmony into ease, strength, harmony and love . . . Indeed this is a time for celebration.

It is time to bid farewell . . . to the cancer cells in your body. You know this . . . and the cancer cells know also . . . They know that the harmony you are calling to your life is not an environment in which they can flourish. They begin to leave your body . . . aura . . . and energy forever! These cancer cells don't suit your life anymore . . . They contain all that is not love . . . all that is connected to disharmony . . . wild growth . . . victimhood . . . lack . . . doubt and suffering. They contain pain, fear, anger . . . sorrow, hardship . . . criticism, self-destruction, self-denial. These distorted cells . . . have lost their inner beauty and centre . . . and no longer reflect your true Self . . . They are appreciated for any good . . . that they may have brought your way . . . but are thanked doubly for moving out of your body and aura . . . Never, ever to return.

Everyone at the party . . . celebrates with you . . . aiding and supporting your farewells . . . Imagine yourself happy, bidding farewell to the cancer cells . . . (using your soul powers . . . with the help of the chemotherapy or other treatments). Thank yourself for knowing . . . that the energy in these cancer cells is not appropriate . . . needed . . . or wanted. Clink glasses in farewell and "see" them leave your body and aura forever.

When you have finished you may enjoy virtual wine with your guests . . . enjoy imagined music and a fantasized, wonderful feast . . . all in pleasant surroundings and happy colours!

GUIDED MEDITATION 6: A PERSONAL PRAYER

You may use my wording, add to it, change it or make your own kind of personal prayer. In a way this prayer expresses how you want your best self to feel. It is a personal prayer that expresses what is felt and plants seeds expressing how you want your future you to feel and live your life. My prayer aims at releasing all that does not support my path to healing. My wording is in the here and now . . . in the present tense . . . like an affirmation or an intention. I use this form consciously since the now is the only time that has the power of creation. You may prepare your own prayer and record it to guide yourself, or just read it to yourself.

Now let's begin:

Find your comfortable position for meditation . . . and place the palms of your hands facing upwards. Gently close your eyes. As you place your attention on your breathing . . . mindfully enter the quiet . . . observe your breath as you breathe in . . . and breathe out . . . as you inhale . . . and exhale. Imagine that with each breath that you are breathing in positive energy . . . energy of light . . . of love . . . of the divine . . . of connectedness. After a few breaths you will find yourself feeling a sense of quiet . . . and calm. Feel the gratitude of connection . . . to your innermost you.

Hear yourself say these words to your inner being,

Today I love and honour me. I am grateful for my presence in this world, for my presence in the divine and for the divine presence in me. I am thankful for my abilities, talents and gifts. My body is strong, balanced and healthy; my soul is filled with joy and tranquillity. I know that all is perfect for my path. My path creates a joyous unity of mind body and soul. All emotions and energies that do not positively contribute to this process are released. As the positive energy of light and love fill each cell of my body, negative energies are released into the earth where they can do no harm to anyone.

I trust that I am in the right place at the right time . . . I express my true self through my intentions and choices . . . I choose love, oneness, joyous relationships, laughter, balance, wonderful health, joyous creativity, passion, giving and receiving, abundance and being all that I can be. I gladly take full responsibility for all that I am . . . and all that I am becoming. As my life fills with joy, I radiate wellbeing onto myself and others . . . I express myself with ease, joy and focus. Balanced giving and receiving enables the abundance in my soul to create abundance around me, as I deserve.

Golden rays of pure love from all that is shine through the crown of my head, flowing through my body to heal and rejuvenate each cell . . . They flow through me and into the earth . . . sprouting roots that stretch throughout the world.

I know I am guided well and am grateful for all guidance given. I honour the unity of my mind, body and soul . . . as I joyously create opportunities to help myself and others.

I am filled with gratitude to the divine – all that is, that is one . . . and I, at one with it. My being, my "I am that I am" . . . surrenders joyfully to divine will to be all that it can be in all that is.

And so it is, and so it is, and so it is.

Amen

GUIDED MEDITATION 7: CHOOSING LIFE

Before undergoing a serious, life-threatening procedure, it's a good idea to be totally present and aware of your desires . . . As I learned through my experience of almost dying, sometimes our passion for life is at low tide. We may feel like what's the use? Maybe I should just let go. I'm so tired of suffering. This reality is not simple. I know how it feels, because I was there and it wasn't easy to look at.

This meditation . . . focuses on uniting all desires towards living and unity. As you unify desires . . . thoughts . . . and feelings before the procedure . . . passion returns . . . focus returns . . . clarity returns . . . This is the time to unify . . . and consciously place yourself wholly in the direction you choose to go. So let's go for it!

Find your comfortable meditation place . . . and gently close your eyes . . . relax the focus of your eyes under your eyelids . . . feel your eyes relax . . . and lose their focus even more . . . Now follow your breathing mindfully . . . aware of inhaling . . . and exhaling . . . aware of the now moment . . . You are just being present . . . just BEING . . . Touch that sense of YOU . . . the you that feels . . . dreams . . . wants . . . is . . . The child you . . . the adolescent you . . . the grownup you . . .

See this YOU blessed with the gift of life . . . Life has its ups and downs . . . Let's look up . . . What do you love about life? What fills you with joy? When do you feel love and bring love into your world? . . . It can be as usual as waking up to a lovely day, making someone else smile . . . laughing out loud . . . running . . . dancing . . . being with family . . . friends . . . See your life fill with opportunities for doing good things . . . loving . . . and being loved . . . and most of all for loving yourself.

Now it is time to nurture your desire . . . with each breath feel all your passion and emotions creating and increasing your desire to live . . . sense the miracle of LIFE itself . . . What a gift! Feel the emotions and desires . . . form powerful thoughts . . . and intentions . . . You have free choice to choose what you want . . .

Hear yourself say to your heart . . . "I choose LIFE" . . . Feel your desire and intention grow as you say to yourself . . . "I choose to create a healthier life . . . and fill it with passion and enjoyment . . . With great gratitude and self-love . . . I choose LIFE . . . I choose Life . . . I choose life . . . I CHOOSE life . . . I CHOOSE LIFE."

Feel how these words and this knowing enter your every breath . . . they enter your lungs . . . your heart . . . your bloodstream . . . flowing to each cell in your body . . . I CHOOSE LIFE . . . enters your DNA. Every cell . . . every molecule in your body has been informed of your conscious unified choice . . . I CHOOSE LIFE. Every molecule . . . every cell chooses with you . . . to adore life . . . to live . . . to be part of a healthy body . . . To let go of any molecules or cells that hinder your health.

Hear yourself whisper to your heart "I CHOOSE LIFE."

"I choose LIFE . . . I CHOOSE life . . . I choose life . . . I choose Life . . . I CHOOSE LIFE."

Feel your total commitment to LIFE . . . and to YOUR LIFE . . .

When you are ready . . . slowly open your eyes . . . and let a big smile express this feeling from the depths of your heart.

GUIDED MEDITATION 8: BONE MARROW TRANSPLANT

Find your comfortable position for meditation . . . and place the palms of your hands facing upwards . . . feel your readiness and openness to receive . . . Gently close your eyes . . . and enter your quiet space . . . Mindfully place your attention on your breathing . . . observe your breath as you breathe in . . . and breathe out . . . as you inhale . . . and exhale . . . Imagine that with each breath you are breathing in positive energy . . . energy of the divine . . . of light . . . of love . . . of connectedness. Exhale the energy of worry and tension . . . After a few breaths find yourself with a sense of quiet . . . and calm . . . feeling the gratitude of being in the quiet . . .

This very special time . . . Can you feel it? You are in the process of creating a new you . . . you are consciously birthing yourself this time . . . resetting the programme for making your blood . . . You are making it new again . . . And this is a gift very few receive. The bone marrow is your essence . . . it is where the body creates the fluid of life . . . your blood. Your new stem cells will become new blood cells . . . new red blood cells to carry nourishment to all your cells . . . new white blood cells to create the cells in your immune system. Stem cells create all blood cells to carry out all the functions that are needed . . . These new cells will create you . . . anew in your bone marrow . . . one of the deepest, most creative parts of your physical body. What a miracle! And how ingenious!

It is time to open to the process of recreating your bone marrow, which means it is time for wonderful decisions. The medical treatment has helped you say goodbye . . . to what did not support your essence in your old bone marrow . . . All the imbalances, emotions . . . behaviours and thoughts showed you what you don't want . . . and thus hinted at what you do want in your life . . . in your essence . . . So let's say goodbye to anything . . . that weakens the essence . . . of the immune system, like: self-criticism . . . anger . . . disharmony . . . aggressiveness . . . cloudy unclear boundaries . . . frustration . . . guilt . . . self-belittling . . . feeling like a victim. Add anything else you wish . . . and imagine these energies leaving your life, your consciousness and your bone marrow with the help of the mega-chemotherapy you are given . . . See this chemotherapy wiping out the old bone marrow . . . making your marrow space available for something new.

Now comes the fun part . . . See your body filled with light and the excitement of the new . . . Imagine all the wonderful qualities you want to come forth in your new bone marrow . . . the new essence of your life creation. Imagine all the things that bring you joy . . . feelings of self-worth . . . and self-love . . . gathering within your consciousness and intentions . . . to fill the essence of your new bone marrow. See the new stem cell transplant rebuilding your essence with healthy . . . unscarred stem cells that have the ability to create health . . . See these new stem cells having clear . . . exacting . . . and beneficial intentions . . . See them balanced and in harmony with life . . . filled with self-love . . . gratitude . . . love . . . joy . . . unity . . . beauty . . . purity . . . good health . . . laughter . . . and smiles. See these qualities as part of the healthy you . . . and your strong, healthy immune system.

Now you can feel focused on knowing what your body is creating . . . You can be happy that your old bone marrow is gone . . . and a new one with new potentials and intentions is taking its place . . . The power and passion of your intentions create a united . . . balanced . . . immune system . . . that functions excellently . . . with love and joy.

And just remember that newborns spend most of their energy on bodybuilding from the cell level . . . so let the process take as long as your body needs it to. Enjoy the process . . . Enjoy new life . . . Enjoy yourself being reborn . . .

When you are ready . . . your can gently open your eyes and smile in gratitude.

GUIDED MEDITATION 9: BONE MARROW (OR ANY) TRANSPLANT FROM A DONOR

Find your comfortable position for meditation . . . Relax your arms . . . turn the palms of your hands upwards . . . declaring your readiness and openness to receive . . . Gently close your eyes . . . and enter your quiet space . . . Mindfully place your attention on your breathing . . . observe your breath as you breathe in . . . and breathe out . . . as you inhale . . . and exhale . . . Imagine that with each breath, you are breathing in positive energy . . . energy of the divine . . . of light . . . of love . . . of connectedness . . . of being in the quiet. Exhale the energy of worry and tension . . . of shadows . . . of isolation. After a few breaths find yourself with a sense of quiet . . . and calm . . . feeling the gratitude of connection to yourself . . .

Feel this very special time . . . You are in the process of creating a new you . . . you are re-birthing yourself . . . resetting the programme . . . And you are able to do this because you have received a precious gift from your donor. This gift . . . healthy donor stem cells . . . will create the blood cells in your bone marrow . . . new red blood cells to carry nourishment to all your cells . . . new white blood cells to create the cells in your immune system and new thrombocytes (platelets) that aid clotting and prevent bleeding. These new cells will create a new you . . . in your bone marrow . . . one of the deepest, most creative parts of your physical body . . . What a miracle! And how ingenious!

Now comes the fun part . . . It is time to open to the process of recreating your bone marrow . . . Which means . . . it is time for wonderful decisions. It is time to know . . . feel . . . all the emotions . . . behaviours and thoughts . . . that you want your new blood cells to have . . . It is time to open yourself to the gift of stem cells that create your body. See your body filled with light and the excitement of the new . . . Imagine all the wonderful qualities you want to manifest with your new bone marrow . . . the new essence of your life creation. Imagine all the things that bring you joy . . . feelings of self-worth . . . and self-love . . . gathering within your consciousness and intentions . . . to fill the essence of your new bone marrow. Imagine the unscarred, newly transplanted stem cells rebuilding your essence with healthy cells . . . that have the ability to create health . . . See these new stem cells having clear . . . exacting . . . and beneficial intentions . . . See them balanced and in harmony with life . . . filled with love . . . gratitude . . . joy . . . unity . . . beauty . . . purity . . . good health . . . laughter . . . and smiles. See these qualities as part of the healthy you . . . and a strong, healthy immune system.

Now let's look closer at your new stem cells . . . at your special gift. They will create the cells that will give power to your immune system . . . to guard you, to keep you safe from invaders. They are new in a strange body. They may not really be sure who's against who in this new body.

Let's introduce ourselves and create a bond between your body and the stem cells so that they will be sure who the good guys are. Imagine the donor stem cells and your cells meeting . . . wondering about each other. They are not 100 per cent alike in their vibration and identity. Now let's go even deeper and look at the molecules of each . . . yes . . . from this level they are a bit more alike . . . Now let's imagine looking even deeper, closer . . . let's reach the atomic and energetic levels . . . All atoms have protons, neutrons and electrons. They vibrate, they have energy . . . Let's see all the atoms fill with light . . . and a sense of cooperation . . . a sense of community. We can now imagine them balancing and finding a way to energetically vibrate in harmony . . . We can see this special bond filling with love on the atomic level . . . see all the atoms . . . from both the graft (donor) and the host (you) honouring each other's existence. Imagine the graft and host becoming great friends . . . lovers . . . family . . . Imagine them knowing they live best in cooperation, helping each other out . . . Feel the joy of nurturing someone you love and accept. Now imagine your atoms, molecules . . . cells feeling that joy, nurturance and acceptance for the stem cells and the stem cells feeling this acceptance and nurturance for the cells in your body.

Imagine a new unity of love filling your immune system . . . from the atomic level upwards. See all your body accepting this energetic bond and trust . . . all the cells . . . yours and your donor's . . . are connected with the desire for a happy, healthy, cooperative body... All is well. And so it is. And so it is.

When you are ready . . . you can gently open your eyes and smile in gratitude.

GUIDED MEDITATION 10: CONTAINING, REDUCING, ERASING TUMOURS

You may choose what you want to do with your tumour. Only what you are ready to release can be effected. I chose containment for my breast tumour . . . That seemed intuitively right for me. Make your intuitive choice or even do all . . . Allowing your body mind to decide.

Find your comfortable position for meditation and with the palms of your hands facing upwards . . . declare your readiness and openness to receive . . . Enter into the quiet . . . mindfully . . . by gently closing your eyes . . . placing your attention on your breathing . . . Observe your breath as you breathe in . . . and breathe out . . . as you inhale . . . and exhale

. . . inhale and . . . exhale . . . Take three deep breaths through your nose . . . and exhale slowly through your mouth . . . Perhaps you can hear your breath as it exits your mouth.

When you feel a sense of quiet . . . and calm . . . imagine that you have an inside view of your physical body like in a science film on the Discovery Channel. You have a wonderful magic wand in your hand to help you do whatever you wish. The first thing you want to do is know what the situation is, so you command your magic wand to search and find the rogue cancer cells throughout your body . . . sort of like searching for a word in a computer program . . . Then tell your magic wand to highlight each rogue cell so that they can easily be seen by your immune system, by the surgeon, by chemotherapy and by your inner knowing.

Imagine that you can perform magic on these highlighted cells . . . you can contain them so they don't spread and can be removed successfully surgically . . . you can try to reduce them so that there is less to remove . . . You may even aim to delete them altogether . . . Just the thought is empowering. Let's try to do all three.

First let's prevent further growth and spreading. Imagine finding the group of rogue cells that form your tumour . . . Now imagine enclosing these cells in an un-escapable clear capsule or a hermetically sealed, clear wrap . . . They are all together with no room to multiply or stray. If we don't want them to get too frenzied and frantic, we can fill the enclosure with sleeping gas to make them fall asleep until the surgeon is ready to take them to tumour-land . . . Wrap any other tumour the same way . . .

If you want to, you can again take your magic wand and imagine it making the tumour/s smaller and smaller. Visualize the tumour shrinking . . . getting smaller . . . and smaller . . . and smaller . . . so it will be easy to get rid of it. Give yourself time to enjoy your imagination . . . feel a smile in your heart . . . enjoy the fun of your own imagination and intentions.

You can also use your magic wand to SELECT the highlighted cells and DELETE them . . . cell by cell . . . by cell or several at a time. Or even waving the magic wand to SELECT ALL physical, behavioural, and emotional cell memories supporting the disharmonic cancer cells . . . Imagine your wand pressing the DELETE ALL button . . . deleting all the cells you are willing to release. See these cells as deleted . . . gone.

This meditation can be repeated as often as you wish . . . When you have completed your "work" . . . it's time to fill the now empty spaces in the body. So let's imagine that there are trillions of tiny Smileys all around you . . . with happy smiling faces ☺, symbols of love . . . self-love . . . kisses. Imagine that with each breath you take . . . the vacant spaces in your body now fill with symbols of love: smiles, hearts, joy and laughter . . . entering each cell from your feet . . . to your shins . . . your knees . . . your thighs . . . your pelvis . . . all your internal organs and spaces up to your waist . . . your chest cavity . . . your hands . . . arms and shoulders . . . your neck . . . your face . . . your head . . . your brain and thoughts . . . your eyes . . . ears . . . mouth . . . gums . . . teeth . . . tongue . . . and finally your lips . . . When you don't have room for anymore emojies it's time to gently open your eyes with a big smile on your face.

GUIDED MEDITATION 11: PREPARATION FOR SURGERY

As you sit in a comfortable position with the palms of your hands open and facing upwards . . . begin to take a few relaxing breaths. Breathe in through your nose . . . and out through your mouth . . . filling yourself with calm and relaxation. Feel your whole body breathe in light and calm and breathe out any discomfort . . . As you breathe in and out . . . You feel calm and quiet filling each and every cell in your body.

Now let's talk to your body . . . It's time to inform all the cells in your body of your decision to have surgery . . . Let your cells know that this is your choice . . . You have agreed and actively want this surgery to help your body function in a better and healthier manner. Tell your cells not to feel punished or that they are being invaded . . . All that is happening to your body is for your greater good. Imagine any worries being easily calmed . . . Your intention for this surgery to succeed in the best possible way is very strong. Tell your cells that they will be put to sleep . . . and should enjoy the slumber. There will be no pain . . . Tell your cells to let the imbalances be taken away . . . removed and that you are happy that they will just go with the flow.

For minimum trauma in the area of the incision ask the cells to open easily to the knife. Ask them to help the grain of the cut to create the least possible scarring. Let the cells know that you intend for them to heal easily without problems . . . Thank them for their cooperation and understanding.

Imagine light glowing from your thoughts and heart . . . filled with your intention for everything to go superbly well . . . Imagine this light filling the operating room with wonderful light energy . . . touching all the instruments, machinery and lighting . . . filling the air . . . filling everything with love and healing energy . . . energy of preciseness and clarity . . . energy of your desire to be the healthiest that you can be. Energy of knowing exactly what to do.

Now see light glowing from your thoughts and heart . . . surround your doctors and nurses with your intentions . . . The light and intentions then merge with them . . . entering their hands . . . their heart . . . their thoughts and mind. Imagine your doctor's hands and mind . . . receiving your light filled with certainty . . . precision . . . and caring. Know that your doctor knows in his or her heart what you want for your body . . . Know that this now has become his or her intention and decision. See golden light surrounding you . . . and know you have done all that you can do.

It is time to just breathe all the good that you wish for yourself . . . calmly and tranquilly and relax . . . And so it is . . . And so it is . . . And so it is.

GUIDED MEDITATION 12: EVERYDAY STANDARD CELL UPGRADE

Find your comfortable meditation place and position . . . and gently close your eyes . . . relax the focus of your eyes under your eyelids . . . feel your eyes relax . . . and lose their focus and relax even more . . . Now follow your breathing mindfully . . . aware of inhaling . . . and exhaling . . . aware of the now moment . . . You are just being present . . . just BEING . . . Touch that sense of YOU . . . the you that feels . . . dreams . . . wants . . . is . . . As you breathe . . . your body feels calmer . . . more peaceful . . . relaxed.

Now imagine yourself in a huge stadium with trillions of seats . . . you can't see all the seats but that doesn't matter. You are on centre stage and the seats are filled with the consciousness of each and every cell . . . organ . . . and molecule in your body. You are so happy to talk to them, and they are ecstatic that you have come to speak to them.

Imagine you, the CEO of your body . . . thanking all your cells for being so loyal to your mind–body. Thank them for supporting your body, your life and creating the physical temple for your soul. Imagine yourself onstage thanking your brain for its ability to think, reason, feel and sense . . . and forming the connections between every part of your body. Imagine thanking each and every nerve in your body for creating the marvellous network of feelings, sensations, creative ideas and rational thoughts. What an amazing system! You feel filled with gratitude and love. For your audience . . . your appreciation is a dream come true.

Now imagine your heart, your circulatory system . . . down to the tiniest capillaries . . . you search them out in the crowd and thank them for their continuous work and the very special nature of the hearts emotional character. Hear yourself express deep gratitude and love. You now thank your digestive system, from the cells in your mouth, and teeth to the large intestine and anus. You thank each cell in every digestive organ . . . that not only digests food, but also emotions and situations . . . You are filled with gratitude and love. Now you look to your reproductive system and thank each cell that creates and nourishes offspring. And your sensory system . . . eyes, nose, tongue, skin, ears, nerves, brain . . . And of course it is time to express gratitude and thanks to your mobility/skeletal system that enables movement, holding, creating, dancing, doing any actions you desire. And of course if you have missed any cells like connective tissue it is time to thank all unknown cells for the part they play in your life. The human body is such a wonder, you feel so blessed.

And now for the game . . . that cells love to play . . . Ask this great audience to send to the stage the most vibrant, vital, well-defined, happy and healthy cell in your entire body . . . There is a stir in the audience . . . Each group looks for their champion and then one representative is chosen by all . . . with love and joy with great anticipation.

Finally one cell comes forward and stands on the stage with you. You hug in joy and love. Now you ask that cell to sing his energy in sound or in colour so that all other cells can tune to it . . . Every cell wants to upgrade itself to the highest level of energy, joy, vitality and health. The chosen cell creates today's standard of excellence. As this wonderful cell sends out his vibration to all the other cells in your body . . . you see a golden mist of energy being absorbed by the cells nearest the stage . . . When they take on this highest vibration they radiate it to other cells close to them . . . Exponentially this golden mist is absorbed in an expanding outwards spiral until all the trillions of cells absorb the golden mist, filled with wonderful energy, joy, vitality, vibrancy, good health, balance and love. You joyously watch how they all tune to the highest vibrations and consciousness of joy and love.

Mmmmm, what a pleasure!

When all the cells are tuned to this new STANDARD you all fill with gratitude and joy . . . You bless all your wonderful cells . . . from your heart . . . There is great excitement and joy throughout your body–mind and soul. Stay in this joy for as long as you wish.

When you are ready you may slowly move your fingers, your toes and then gently open your eyes and let a joyous smile form on your lips.

NOTE

1. I read about this idea of using a standard cell meditation on the Crimson Circle website some time before I became ill (2007). I find it very useful. Get more information at www.crimsoncircle.com.

Chapter 22
Creating Personalized Visualizations

We have all seen athletes "psyching themselves up" before they compete. You can see the concentration. What are they doing? They visualize their goal, see themselves succeeding, and "feel" themselves reach their goal as completely and with as much detail as possible. They create the potential they desire and see themselves there – feel themselves there to optimize their potentials. Here follows some simple guidelines for manifesting your visualizations.

- Intentions create: Look clearly at what you want before starting out. Choose a clear intention that reflects what you want and imagine it being fulfilled.

- Thoughts create biology and chemistry: We are always talking directly to our biology. Sometimes we even hear it talk back. This is scientific fact. For example, the thought that we see a snake in a bush near us is enough to set off a stream of creations – from behavioural reactions to a chain of biological and chemical responses like increased heart beat, increased oxygen to peripheral muscles, and adrenal hormones setting off a chain of reaction called our basic "fight or flight" response. Emotions like fear, anxiety, joy and tranquillity create different chemical reactions, hormonal secretions, electrical impulses creating muscle reactions, etc. The detrimental effects of anxiety and stress on the body are mainstream knowledge. In contrast, the positive effects of meditation, joy, love and laughter have a balancing effect and are known to enhance the body's immune system and stabilize various physiological factors. This is the way the body works

- Nature creates mechanisms to support life: To nature, birth, flourishing, decay and death are parts of the same on-going process – in plants, animals, our species, our cells, parts of our cells. Whether the result is health or sickness, nature expresses its mechanisms. As scientific research reveals new understandings about the biology of life, the cell, and how diseases work, ideas are created for sophisticated solutions. We can use these understandings even before the drug is available by using the theory behind them as visualization right now . . . Information is frequently available on the Internet with images, animations and sometimes lectures. There are many images and scientific facts that can be used to let the body know what you want.

For example, recently I heard a fascinating lecture and slide presentation about research regarding multiple myeloma (bone marrow cancer). The myeloma cancer cells are abnormal plasma cells created to fight off a non-existent threat. Natural mechanisms keep these cancer cells growing, living and reproducing, creating a way for its inappropriate behaviour to go unrecognized by the immune system. The myeloma cells attach themselves to bone marrow cells to stimulate the creation of a kind of glue encouraging the growth of roots for nourishment and an increasingly supportive environment. The research presented involved finding a way to block the environmental support by aiming at the glue that roots the myeloma cells to the bone marrow. I was elated. It didn't matter to me if there was such a drug or not. I had been given a clue to the mechanism that supported the cancer cells' life and I could use that image against it. Images and knowledge are part of my conversations with my cells. Check out information about your condition with the aim of being an imagery detective.

Try the following guided imagery to see how it works when we put it all together:

1. Enter a relaxed state and into the now moment by concentrating your attention on your breath. Slow down and feel your conscious attention with every moment of your in-breath and out-breath. The now moment is the place of power. Be with what is now. Then use the image that expresses the solution you want as the core of your guided imagery.

2. Imagine you are inside your body with a beautiful coloured magic wand.

3.   Your wand spreads GLUE DISSOLVER and the beautiful colour over all your affected parts of your body.

4.   Watch how the glue is joyously dissolved and how the cancer cells' support system is disconnected.

5.   Observe how the cancer cells shrivel and die when they are without life support.

6.   See the healthy cells rejoice.

7.   Thank your body and all your cells for having so much fun with you.

Another example comes from my mom. When she had the chemo inside her bladder she imagined the cancer cells all red-brown and nasty. Slowly she "saw" the chemo wash them clean until they were filled with light and transparent like the healthy cells.

Whatever positive thought or idea enters your imagination can be envisioned as part of the way your body is talking to you and you can use it in your visualizations however you like. Enjoy being creative.

Chapter 23
Creative Tips

As mentioned earlier in the book, drawing and painting are activities that almost all of us are familiar with, even if we have not done anything in that area since childhood. Talent is not the emphasis in these drawings, the doing is. I have seen the joy and relaxation of so many patients in the hospitals I work in when I pass out drawing materials and mandalas to colour. In most places supplies are readily available and in many price ranges, too. Here are some ideas for your "to buy" wish list.

Suggested Thought Work supply list:

- Journal, notebook or writing paper.

- Pencil or pen to write or draw with. (2B, B5 and B8 drawing pencils if you like working in graphite pencil. I also enjoy drawing with simple mechanical pencils.)

- Drawing paper: Block of white, heavy drawing paper, good for both drawing and watercolours (at least 180–200 grams or more). Optional: black or coloured paper to use with white and coloured pencils and pens.

- Coloured pencils: You may like regular oil-based pencils or aquarelle based. I personally prefer the aquarelle coloured pencils, which are water soluble, because they are easy to work with and work well with watercolours. There are many brands available so here's a rule of thumb: the softer they are, the easier they spread, the grainier the texture, the less sharp they sharpen and the easier they break. The very inexpensive ones may be too hard and some artist grade may be too soft for your personal feel. I like something in the middle. Try to test them before you choose. Look for a nice variety – at least 24 different colours – but the more the merrier.

- Pencil sharpener and eraser.

- Watercolours: There are various qualities available, from "kids" watercolour sets to high-quality artist sets. The difference is in price, colours, pigment quality, intensity and colour saturation. And yes there is a real difference. Watercolour can come in tubes or cakes (pans). Pan sets usually come in metal boxes with a cover that serves as a palette for mixing colours. If you buy tubes, get yourself a nice sized palette with lots of separations and a lid so you can close the pallet and save your colour array to reuse leftover, dried colour. Gold and silver watercolour tubes can be bought separately and are mixable with any watercolour to get metallic colour mixes.[1]

- Watercolour brushes: These come in two basic categories: round (for lines) and flat (for broader surfaces) and in various widths as numbered. If you buy a good set of watercolours a brush may be included.

- Use a container or cup with clean water to wet paint and rinse brushes. Remember to change the water when it gets dirty and to clean your brush before touching a new colour.

- Pens: Permanent ink and/or gel-tip pens come in a variety of colours, glitters and metallic shades and are great for accents and special touches. I personally love to use the metallic shades and glitter shades to add a healing touch.

- Felt-tip pens: I like permanent archival Indian ink pens for drawing and as outlines and details when working with watercolours because they don't bleed. Pens can be found in different colours, different widths and even with a brush tip. Coloured felt-tip pens can be water soluble like those sold in multicolour sets or permanent markers, like Indian ink pens, and also come with a variety of widths and tips, and are sold individually or in sets.

- A lockable compass (enabling the radius to be fixed at a particular size).

- A ruler (preferably transparent).

Optional:

- Light a candle and or incense when meditating, journaling, drawing, any time.

- I love to hear calm soothing music playing in the background and I love silence. It's a matter of taste, preference, availability, etc.

USING WATERCOLOURS

Although watercolour is less controllable than pens and pencils, working in watercolour is wonderful for expressing feelings and emotions. Unlike poster paint, watercolours are transparent to a degree and are not meant create one flat, unified surface. A patch of watercolour can reveal interesting textures and colour blends. Be on the lookout. The wetness or dryness as well as the amount of colour on the brush create variations. Other effects result from varying brush strokes (how the paint is brushed on the paper), degrees of transparencies (high quantities of water add transparency and make colour appear lighter) and blends. Colours may be blended by painting over a dried layer of paint or adding a colour to another wet colour on the paper. All this adds depth and richness. You can push the paint around, vary where it is heavier or lighter with pigment, let colours meet and spread into one another . . . let a drop of colour touch the wet surface of another colour and see what happens. It's fun to explore.

You may want to play systematically, taking only a small amount of paint on the wet brush and then vary the amount of colour and water on the brush to see a range of effects and possibilities. You can also play with the paper. Watercolour reacts differently on dry paper than on wet paper. Compare the effect by taking some clean water on a brush to wet an area of the paper, while leaving other areas dry. Then use a brush with colour on both the wet and dry paper. Examine the effects, where and when the paint spreads. Be careful not to rub the paper too much when it is wet because some paper can tire and peel.

Remember to rinse your brush in water before touching another colour on your pallet so your colours remain pure. If you don't see the colour you want, mix the colour with another colour on your palette. When mixing colours, you have more control when you add a drop of the darker colour to a lighter colour and not the reverse. To make a colour light without losing transparency and intensity, dilute the colour by adding more water. You can also get a lighter colour by adding white, however the colour will lose transparency.

Coloured pencils can be applied one colour on top of the other for interesting blends and shading. For example yellows and reds will create an orangey effect, blues and reds will create a purple effect and yellows and blues create green. Mixing any two or three colours will add richness.

If you use a wet brush on an area coloured by aquarelle pencils, the wet pencil pigment will blend like watercolour. Sometimes that's good and sometimes the result may look muddy, depending on what you want and what colours are blending. It's interesting to use pencils while working with watercolours for details or on wet paper to draw lines, designs, etc. You also can "erase" things on purpose (like growths) by dissolving the colour in water and absorbing it with a tissue – which may be just what you want to do.

You may also try white and coloured pencils on black paper or coloured construction paper. When drawing with a white pencil on black paper you are drawing the light and not the shadow, which is what we are used to doing. It's a lovely way to raise your attention to the light around you. You can colour with coloured pencils on the white area and directly on the black. Results are very impressive.

HOW TO DRAW² 1: THE SEED OF LIFE MANDALA

1. Place the compass point in the centre of the page

2. Open the compass to a radius of 3.5cm and draw a circle around that point

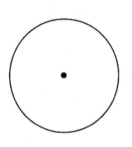

3. Place the compass point at the upper edge of the circle and create a second circle with the same size radius

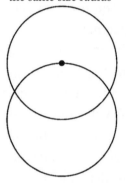

4. Make a third circle whose centre is the right intersecting point of the two circles

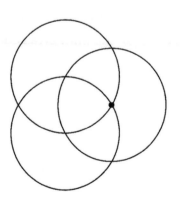

5. Make a fourth circle from the third intersection point

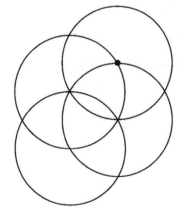

6. Make a circle from the next intersection of the circles

7. Make a circle from the next intersection of the circles

8. Make a circle from the next intersection of the circles, completing the template

Seed of Life Mandala template

HOW TO DRAW 2: THE FLOWER OF LIFE MANDALA

1. Open the compass to a radius of 3.5cm and draw the seed of life template as per the previous instructions

2. Mark the six outer intersection points with a pencil and draw circles around each marked dot

3. Mark the six new intersection points with a pencil and draw a circle around each marked dot

4. Draw two large circles with the compass with 0.5cm distance between them to frame the interlaced circles

Flower of Life template

HOW TO DRAW 3: THE MANDALA OF TWELVE

1. Draw a circle with a radius of 3.5 cm. Mark the centre as point 0.

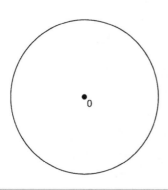

2. Place the compass at the upper most point of the circle, point 1, and divide the circle into 6 equal parts by using the compass radius to mark points 2–6

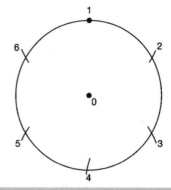

3. Place the compass point at point 2 and mark a small arc outside the circle opposite the 0. Place the compass point at point 3 and intersect the arc with another arc and mark it as point 7. Using a ruler connect point 7 to point 0 and mark line 8–9

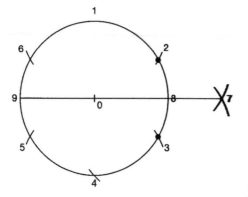

4. Place the point of compass (with the same radius opening) on point 8 and mark point 10 and point 11 on the circle. Place the compass on point 9 and mark points 12 and 13

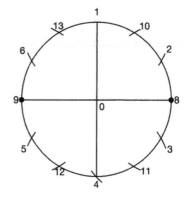

5. From each point on the circle draw a new circle with the same radius

The TWELVE Template

NOTES

1. Blue + silver = metallic blue; gold + red= copper.
2. Templates and instructions are taken from Eitan Kedmy's wonderful book, *Mandala Way*, which has a wealth of information on these and other mandala templates as well as mandalas in general. Eitan Kedmy is a talented artist and good friend who led a workshop on mandalas that I attended a few years before I became ill. Today I teach mandala drawing using his method. In his book, which I translated from Hebrew to English, he not only teaches 18 different mandala formats and their meanings, he discusses mandala history, meanings and many ways to interpret the mandalas you draw. I highly recommend his beautifully illustrated book to all art and mandala lovers.

Appendix I

More on the Law of Attraction

Esther and Jerry Hicks (www.Abraham-hicks.com) have written many books about the Law of Attraction[1] and how to use it and live by it. I recommend them highly. There are also endless free YouTube discussions of various topics and the Law of Attraction. Just look up Abraham-Hicks on the Internet. Below I very briefly discuss the three basic components for manifesting reality, as I understand it.

ASK AND IT SHALL BE GIVEN . . .

The first law – ASK: requests are energetically communicated to the universe. We ask verbally and nonverbally by placing our attention, thoughts, feelings and prayers on something or simply stating our desires. The more we place our attention and focus on the same thought, in general or with specificity and detail, the more dominant the thought becomes and the stronger its potential to manifest or become real. Emotion and passion adds to the energy of the request.

The second law – IT SHALL BE GIVEN – is about the universe's response: the universe receives our request and always responds positively by setting energy and synchronicity into motion. Of course, if we send mixed messages we get mixed answers that may cancel each other out (for example, "I want . . . but . . . "). If we send emotionally weak requests . . . we get weak answers. If we send a wanting . . . like "I want to be rich" . . . we get the wanting to be rich. So just like with affirmations, it is important to request something in a positive, present form, just like you are sowing the seeds.

The third law regards ALLOWING: this is the hardest part. It is our responsibility and challenge to allow ourselves to receive. Why aren't we all rich and beautiful, etc.? The hitch is that we are only able to receive whatever is an energetic or vibrational match to our present energy or vibration – hence LIKE ATTRACTS LIKE. We have to be tuned in to the vibration of joy if we want to experience joy. If I want to listen to jazz on the radio and I am tuned in to the frequency of a 24/7 news station, there is no way I am going to hear jazz. I have to be tuned to the right station. As I understand it, a dominant feeling or thought of joy attracts situations for joyfulness. If you are predominantly angry or don't believe you deserve to be happy, you aren't tuned into the frequency of joy. You are tuned in for more situations to express anger. If we try to attract joy, or money or health, but are filled with anger or disappointment or plain wanting, we attract only what we radiate – what we are tuned to – which would be situations that energetically match anger, disappointment and wanting.

We are responsible for laws 1 and 3 – for asking as positively, clearly and unequivocally as we can in the present tense, and to be open and tuned to receive it. Deliberate, conscious creation entails being aware of our state of mind, our thoughts and desires, and tuning our feelings or basic emotional frequencies to match the energy of what we request. That usually means doing things to raise our vibration to one of joy, love and wellbeing.

I knew that my golden path would reflect what I was able to receive . . . I was only limited by my own ability to accept joy, love and wellbeing. Our energetic level is a reflection of the emotions that fill our now and I needed mine to match a feeling, frequency or vibration of being on a golden path. That's what "like attracts like" means. If I wanted to attract joy and ease to pave my path, I had to be tuned to energy that matched joy and ease . . . I had to "be" with joy and ease now.

Appendix II
More About the Placebo and Nocebo Effects

There was a time when the placebo effect or response was considered a problem that messed up research, especially for pharmaceutical companies, because it showed that the medication or treatment was no better than "a sugar pill". The placebo effect or response is a measureable, positive effect that "something", other than the treatment being tested, has on the patient's health, whether it be a sugar pill that is thought to be a real medication, the expectations of the doctor or a written article that the medical protocol is an effective healing possibility, or even sham surgery that is thought to be real surgery. All these and more have been tested in scientific research upholding the highest standards. Many authors and scientists have come to the conclusion that it isn't a mess-up at all. It is "something" to be researched, understood and used to support healing potentials. A patient's positive or negative beliefs affect their healing potentials.

The nocebo response is the opposite of the placebo response and can be triggered by negative expectations, knowing and perhaps expecting the side effects of treatments or ideas that negatively influence healing potentials . . . like my mom's doctor who didn't believe the chemo treatment would kill all the cancer. For anyone interested in the research behind these phenomena, there are about 2,650,000 online results for research on the placebo effect. Among them:

harvardmagazine.com/2013/01/the-placebo-phenomenon
www.health.harvard.edu/mind-and-mood/putting-the-placebo-effect-to-work
www.wrf.org/alternative-therapies/power-of-mind-placebo.php
https://allabouttheplaceboeffect.wordpress.com/key-facts-and-statistics/

There are also many books that deal with this subject, for example:

You Are the Placebo: *Making your Mind Matter* by Dr Joe Dispenza;
Mind Over Medicine: *Scientific Proof that You Can Heal Yourself* by Lissa Rankin, MD
The Intention Experiment by Lynn McTaggart
Beyond the Relaxation Response, by Herbert Benson, MD

Appendix III

Organization Charts and Other Tips

These are my Gadi pages that I used to restart my life after my bone marrow transplant.

LIFE-WORK FORMAT CHART

The following template shows how you can use a work format chart to organize goals in all areas of life: health, work, emotions, spirituality, attitudes, art and anything else. Write what you need to do, or be open to in each area. Be specific.

Body – Health	Work	Emotions	Spirituality	Attitudes	Social life	?

WEEKLY CREATORSHIP PAGES

Weekly list to include:
- Gratitude – list everything that you felt grateful for this past week.
- Dids – what you did this past week in the various areas of your life – you can take it from your work chart: building your spirit, health, your body, your work, etc.
- I will's – what will you do this coming week in the various areas of your life – work chart: building your spirit, health, your body, your work, etc.
- Help you need – in any area.
- Help you gave – in any area.
- Visualizations – dream big and let the stars be the limit.

NOTE

1. See *The Teachings of Abraham, The Amazing Power of Deliberate Intent* and *Ask and It Shall Be Given,* by Esther and Jerry Hicks which explains in great detail how we can manifest what we want in reality and what we can do to tune ourselves to allow ourselves to receive easily.

Bibliography and Suggested Reading

Chopra, Deepak. *Ageless Body, Timeless Mind*. New York: Harmony Books, 1993

—— *Journey Into Healing*. New York: Harmony, 1994

—— *Quantum Healing: Exploring the Frontiers of Mind/Body Medicine*. New York: Bantam Books, 1989

—— *Reinventing the Body, Resurrecting the Soul*. New York: Three Rivers Press, 2009

Chopra, Deepak, and David Simon. *Grow Younger, Live Longer*. New York: Harmony Books, 2001

Clark, Dawn E. *Gifts for the Soul*. USA: Infinte Energylinks, Inc., 1999–2001

Cornell, Ann Weiser. *The Power of Focusing*. New York: MJF Books, 1990

Dalai Lama and Berzin, Alexander. *The Gelug/Kagyu Tradition of Mahamudra*. Ithaca, NY, Snow Lion Publications, 1997

Edwards, Betty. *Drawing on the Right Side of the Brain*. New York: Tarcher, 1989

Emoto, Masaru. *The Hidden Messages in Water*. Hillsboro, OR: Beyond Words Publishing, 2001

Gendlin, Eugene T. *Focusing*. New York: Bantam Books, 1981

Hawkes, Joyce Whiteley. *Cell-Level Healing*. New York: Atria Books, 2006

Hay, Louise L. *Heal Your Body: The Mental Causes for Physical Illness and the Metaphysical Way to Overcome Them*. Carlsbad, CA: Hay House, 1982

—— *You Can Heal Your Life*. Santa Monica, CA: Hay House, 1984

Hicks, Esther, and Jerry Hicks. *Ask and It is Given*. Carlsbad, CA: Hay House, 2004

—— *The Amazing Power of Deliberate Intent*. Carlsbad, CA: Hay House, 2006

Jung, Carl G. *Man and His Symbols*. New York: Laurel books, 1964

—— *Mandala Symbolism*. Princeton, NJ: Princeton University Press, 1969

—— *Memories, Dreams, Reflections*. New York: Vintage Books, 1989

Katie, Byron. *A Thousand Names for Joy*. New York: Harmony Books, 2007

—— *Loving What Is*. New York: Three Rivers Press, 2002

Kedmy, Eitan. *The Mandala Way*. Tel Aviv: Bindu, 2010 (Hebrew)

—— *The Mandala Way*. Tel Aviv: Bindu, 2012 (English)

Lipton, Bruce H. *The Biology of Belief*. Carlsbad, CA: Hay House, 2005

McTaggart, Lynne. *The Field*. London: Element, 2003

—— *The Intention Experiment*. New York: Free Press, 2007

Murakami, Haruki. *What I Talk About When I Talk About Running*. London: Vintage Books, 2008

Nelson, Bradley. *The Emotion Code*. Mesquite, NV: Wellness Unmasked Publishing, 2007

Pert, Candace B. *Molecules of Emotion*. New York: Scribner, 1997

Ruiz, Don Miguel. *The Four Agreements*. San Rafael, CA: Amber-Allen Publishing, 1997

Siegel, Bernie S. *Love, Medicine & Miracles*. London: Arrow Books, 1988

Tolle, Eckhart. *A New Earth*. New York: Plume, 2005

—— *The Power of Now*. Vancouver, Canada: Namaste Publishing, 1999

MORE SUGGESTED READING

Benson, Herbert, MD. *Beyond the Relaxation Response*. New York: Berkley Books, 1985

Dispenza, Joe. *You Are the Placebo: Making your Mind Matter*. Carlsbad, CA: Hay House, 2014

Rankin, Lissa, MD. *Mind Over Medicine: Scientific Proof that You Can Heal Yourself*. Carlsbad, CA: Hay House, 2013

FAVOURITE MEDITATION MUSIC ARTISTS

Robert H. Coxon – I use his *Prelude to Infinity* for my guided meditations

Steven Halpern – Music my mother used with subconscious healing messages.

Acknowledgements

I thank the medical staff of Assaf Harofe and Tel Hashomer hospitals who cared for me so well … and especially Dr Naomi Rahimi-Levine.

I thank all my friends and family who were there for me during those good and bad times and to all those who participated in my virtual parties and festivals sending me wonderful energy. I know it made a difference.

I thank all those who gave their comments, advice, criticism, encouragement and support to help me find the best way to get my message across and turn my book into a reality. Special thanks to Marge Silvestri, Leah Frishberg, Yehoram and my miracle-loving friend Rachel.

And, last but not least, I wish to thank the kind people at Watkins Publishing for their help, understanding and expertise transforming my writing into a physical book … May it reach everyone who can benefit from its words.